# CONFLICT ANALYSIS TRAINING

## A Program of Emotional Education

**Albert J. Levis, M.D., Director,**

**Center for the Study of Normative Behavior**

**Institute of Conflict Analysis**



Normative Publications, Manchester Village, Vermont 05254

ISBN: 0-929642-01-5

Library of Congress Catalogue Number: 88-090913

FIRST EDITION 1988

First Printing, 5000 copies

Manufactured in the United States of America

NORMATIVE PUBLICATIONS, Institute of Conflict Analysis, Manchester Village, Vermont 05254

## NORMATIVE PUBLICAITONS, THE FORMAL MANIFESTO JOURNAL, AND THE INSTITUTE OF CONFLICT ANALYSIS

### Rationale for a Publishing Venture, a Journal and an Independent Learning Center:

Theoretical positions usually establish their own linguistic-conceptual communities, that is, their own following of scholars who are willing to communicate in the particular language of a theoretical system. **The Normative Publications, the Formal Manifesto Journal** and the **Institute of Conflict Analysis** were created to facilitate the development and service the needs of an emerging community that will understand, explore, research, and communicate in the novel language of the upcoming numerous formal theoretical publications.

### The Publications, the Journal and the Institute are Dedicated to the Promotion of a New Conceptualization and of a New Psychological Testing Technology:

The creation of this Publishing House, the Journal, and the Training Center to accompany the formal publications is imperative because (1) the formal conceptualization, (2) the testing technology and (3) the theory related service delivery concept constitute three distinct departures from traditional languages and professional discipline role definitions. The function of the Publications and of the Institute of Conflict Analysis is to promote the advancement of the formal theoretical perspective. The Institute will serve the standardization of the delivery of emotional education programs.

### The Publications and the Institute Address a New Constituency:

It may be expected that Conflict Analysis will bring about the integration of interdisciplinary knowledge and the reconciliation of all students of behavior, humanities, and science majors into a conceptually unified constituency. Thus the formal theoretical perspective will put a halt both to the proliferation of schools of thought and to the fragmentation of the scholarly public. This theoretical develepent will contribute in the introduction of the scientific study of conflict into the higher educational institutions, the recognized, established, and accredited academic centers. The Publications, the Journal and the Manchester Institute of Conflict Analysis are needed to channel the new scholarship to a new coalition of scholars consisting of scientists, psychotherapists, educators, people managers, artists, as well as the general public.

**For inquiries regarding the Journal, the Institute's Educational Programs and the Normative Publications:**

**Call 800- 648-4944Vermont 802-362-2500/802-362-2216.Write to: P.O.Box 468 Manchester Village, Vermont, 05254**

# TABLE OF CONTENTS

# INFORMED CONSENT FOR THE ACCEPTANCE OF PERSONAL RESPONSIBILITY FOR THE TRAINING PROCESS

The **Conflict Analysis Training**, is an emotional educational program based on **Dr. A. J. Levis' Conflict Analysis - The Formal Theory of Behavior**. The training consists of four segments: lectures, testing, self-processing of the tests, and finally sharing of the information. The objectives of the training are to learn about behavior and find out about one's relational patterns, how one communicates with others. There is a corrective component in this training program. The training represents an educational program about behavior focusing on the dialectic processes of conflict resolution. Within either a therapeutic or a purely educational setting, the training provides a concise personalized emotional education program.

The **Conflict Analysis Battery** consists of an inventory, several art tasks, and associated questionnaires, a new breed of projective psychological techniques. These tests help to accumulate personal information and to analyze it projectively, which leads to the demonstration of how one deals with stress creatively using the **Conflict Resolution Process**. The testing format helps to integrate information meaningfully. Early experiences of passivity are connected to current reactive patterns of mastery. Both passivity and mastery behaviors manifest in the series of documents the testee creates and then evaluates. The testee finally integrates this information into a continuous pattern of evolution. Information from the lectures and insights from the testing will help you corroborate composing a letter to oneself, the "Know Thyself Statement," in which a person accepts responsibility for one's relational shortcomings and recognizes the direction for changes.

The entire process is intellectually and emotionally demanding, but also extremely rewarding. The testee creates an artistic statement, releases pent up emotions, organizes his/her ideas, and may share and discuss the protocols within a group setting with the objectives to verify the correctness of self-assessments, to identify the degree of conflict, to achieve communicational breakthroughs, and to develop responsible self-awareness about one's attitude. The training represents an educational program about behavior focusing on the dialectic processes of conflict resolution.Within either a therapeutic or a purely educational setting, the training provides a concise personalized emotional education program.

It is possible that a testee, by oneself, or with assistance, identify serious pathology or simply areas of weakness in which he/she needs assistance. We recommend that he/she seek this assistance from a properly trained educator or therapist. Counseling and therapy expedite the spontaneous conflict resolution processes helping to attain effective communicational patterns. This training facilitates the development of insights, occasionally it has therapeutic functions, but the transition from intellectual insight to restructuring of relations, is more difficult to attain than achieving insights alone.

There are emotional and social risks when one deals with issues of one's own conflict, especially when revealing one's conflicts.Usually the conflicted person exaggerates the impact of his/her misconduct and is relieved by its admission - but this is not always the case. So you have to use your own discretion in revealing your testing to others. When in doubt or in pain, you are encouraged to seek assistance. This is especially recommended if you feel vulnerable, unresolved, depressed, listless, or angry.

Participation in this educational program is elective. Participants may withdraw from the study at any time. Before you initiate this testing and training program, you should sign in the space below indicating that you are cognizant of the emotional nature and social ramifications of this process and that you accept the responsibility for any mental anguish you might experience in the process of its completion.

**Informed Consent:**

I have been informed about possible adverse reactions to this process and I accept responsibility for protecting myself from adverse emotional reactions.

Signature______________________________

Date__________________________________

Witness_______________________________

**Information on the potential publication of this work:**

The completed CAT record frequently is of both literary and scientific value. Therefore it could be useful both as a literary development and for scientific research. The ensuing document being composed both by the author of the battery (Dr. A. Levis) and yourself (the testee) is legally regarded as joint property. In order for all or part of your CAT to be published, both authors must come to a satisfactory agreement protecting their interests as authors. It is suggested, in principle, that for scientific studies of the testing, and when the record is held by an academic or clinical institution, that both the author of the record and the author of the testing provide release for reproduction. It is also suggested that the testee grant this right to the clinician or researcher at this point by signing both the consent and the release statements.

**Release to the Clinician to use this Record for Scientific Research:**

I grant permission that my records be used for research purposes and that art and text may be reproduced, provided my identity is concealed.

Signature___________________________

Date______________________________

Witness____________________________

# INTRODUCTION TO CONFLICT ANALYSIS TRAINING

The objective of **Conflict Analysis Training (CAT)** is one of emotional education for the public. This objective is reached through four instruments: a series of lectures, the self-assessment testing, analytical processes, and skills development exercises. It is administrable in flexible formats of delivery adjusted for age, time alotted, and needs addressed.

The core of the program is: First, a series of lectures advancing a coherent theory of behavior and communications, and second, a bundle of psychological self-assessment testing, including an inventory test, artwork exercises, and related analytical and synthetic processes, through which the testee analyzes his/her relational pattern and explores choices for self-improvement.

The testing is an application and demonstration of the theory. The combination of an educational program with a psychological testing experience integrates knowledge with insight, that is, self-knowledge. The testee is a student, and the testing process consolidates learning with growth. A person receives clarity about behavior, and simultaneously about oneself. Both the testing and education have been acclaimed as the state-of-the-art in the state of the science.

The educational focus of this program is to understand the engineering of relational systems and the physics of conflict resolution processes. Included in this concise learning experience are definitions of constructs and the presentation of formulas on matters of behavior. The trainee first understands the cyclic nature of role systems, the importance of cooperative relating, of moderation and the free flow of communications to attain effectiveness and then measures, through the testing, his/her own relational dimensions. The personal diagnostic function of the training consists in attaining integration of information about oneself and identifying directions for change.

The training as part of educational programs introduces the relevance of self-knowledge, as part of therapy, it gives the person accrued awareness of his/her relational pattern, it integrates the individual's disparate symbolic transformations into a meaningful system with clear objectives to pursue in the course of therapy. The training workbook becomes a record of personal growth, especially when it is readministered periodically to a given population. It serves to enhance and to monitor developmental growth

Independently of its educational and its growth facilitating functions, the production of the art and the text of the testing leads to the appreciation of creativity as a legitimate form of self expression. Participation in the program regularly helps to raise awareness of creativity's importance toward more complete expression of one's feelings.

Because of the training's powerful, insightful, emotional, and educational features, its diagnostic and therapeutic qualities, the training is of relevance in various clinical and institutional settings. It belongs as emotional education in the classroom, as effectiveness promoting in the workplace. It may be used for pre-employment screening and for post-employment training. As a diagnostic and therapeutic instrument, it is useful in inpatient and outpatient facilities. As a cost effective, non-intrusive, non-demanding program, it may be helpful at correctional institutions, and drug and alcohol rehabilitation programs. The psychological tests may be administered individually independantly of the comprehensive training program.

This training experience offers significant intellectual, emotional, and social growth. It makes the "Know Thyself" educational imperative finally a realistic and highly attainable goal.

# CONFLICT ANALYSIS TRAINING THROUGH THE LEVIS METAPHOR ANALYSIS PROCESS

The objective of this training is double. The first is educational, to learn the principles of the science of behavior. The second is personal emotional growth achieved as the trainee experiences reduction of conflict through communicating emotions and organizing thoughts in the process of completing the testing and the training process.

The information on behavior is based on Dr. Levis' **Conflict Analysis - The Formal Theory of Behavior.** The theory related self-assessment tests are called the **Conflict Analysis Battery.** The process of this delivery is called **Conflict Analysis Training through the Formal Analysis of Metaphors** or the **Levis Metaphor Analysis Process.**

The Conflict Analysis Training consists of four segments: The first is didactic. The task here is to impart clarity on understanding behavior as a science. This is achieved through **a series of lectures** on , or a single abbreviated presentation of **Conflict Analysis Theory**. The lecture series is referred to as **Conflict Analysis Lecture Series (CALS)**. The second segment is diagnostic. It consists of completing a thorough self-assessment battery, the **Conflict Analysis Battery (CAB).** The task is for the trainee to be creative and to interprete his art work. The third segment is interpretive and integrative. It is the **Formal Role Analysis Process(FRAP)** which leads a person to explore the significance of the information gathered through the testing battery toward actually learning to recognize patterns, their origination, and their obligatory recurrence. During the fourth segment, **Relational Pattern Modification, or Formal Analysis Skills Training (FAST),** the trainee seeks to identify the current recurrence of his or her relational pattern in the training related interpersonal transactions. This pattern is observed as affecting the effective completion of the workshop. In the light of information derived from the protocols, the trainee accepts responsibility for introducing distortions leading to conflict or resistance to change. These conflicts are detected, analyzed ,and hopefully effectively dealt with during this, the final phase of the training. Introspectiveness and willingness to communicate effectively are the new skills acquired in this part of training.

## Section #1 The Theory: Conflict Analysis Lecture Series (CALS)

The educational segment focuses on imparting information on a new theory: **Conflict Analysis - The Formal Theory of Behavior.** Conflict means any and every way a person structures relations, that is, how a person relates to others. Conflict is viewed as a natural science phenomenon completely illustrated through the phenomenon of an oscillating pendulum studied in physics as the **Simple Harmonic Motion (SHM)**. Physics' pendulum constructs and formulas are equivalent to concepts and correlations pertinent to the field of behavioral phenomena. The individual as the pendulum ball at any instant has a particular position (S), velocity (v), and acceleration (a) or social power position (S), activity state (v), and feelings (a). These constructs enter in formulas that determine predictable patterns of transformations that occur in the natural phenomenon of the oscillating pendulum, as well as in the realm of phenomena of conflict.

A series of ten levels of analysis corresponding each to a formula from physics, logic, and mathematics, **The Formal Analysis Profile (FAP), provides the guidelines for the comprehensive analysis of relational phenomena.** Accordingly, conflicts constitute ideational systems that have quantifiable parameters or dimensions. (Levels 1-2). The essence of conflict is energy (Level 3), this energy is conserved through energetic transformations (Level 4) i.e., potential to kinetic or psychic to social or action energy. The individual , just like the pendulum, is characterized by the qualification of efficiency in these energetic transformations (Level 10). Energy is released, the oscillation stops when the individual ceases to be conflicted, i.e., when he/she releases the feeling - energy related to some experience and when he/she resolves conflict by compromising with painful realities rather than being defensive about them.

## Section # 2 Self Assessment Testing: The Conflict Analysis Battery

To measure personal dimensions, that is, in order to evaluate or assess a person's conflict resolution process, including relational pattern, energies, intertransformations, fixations of energies, etc., we observe a person's mental oscillations as manifestations of his/her pendulum in motion. An excellent system of mental oscillations is generated and processed under the Conflict Analysis Battery of Metaphors; these tests corroborate to identify the person's symbolic universe and to reveal the order of ideas within it.

**The Conflict Analysis Battery** consists in the systematic production of art and text metaphors, that is, of ministructures of personal patterns of conflict.

A distinct feature of the CAB testing is its self-assessment objective. The pattern revealed in the metaphors is assessed by the testee. He or she is the sole recipient, interpreter, and beneficiary of the insights derived from the testing.

The testing process leads from the intuitive production of unconsciously significant configurations to their systematic analysis. Gradually the unconscious becomes conscious. A person understands, through interpreted metaphors, personal patterns of conflict generation and resolution and comes to suggestions of what changes he/she has to make to improve on these patterns. Insights are reached intuitively as one recognizes how one communicates or relates to others. The testee rediscovers the key relational concerns throughout the testing consistently in every metaphor. The Formal Questionnaire Process facilitates the individual to identify in the characters of the metaphor complementary aspects of his/her world. Gradually, in the mutual exchanges of these two separate figures, one recognizes one's own complete personal relational universe. The CAB includes the following tests:

**The Relational Modality Evaluation Scale (RMES)**

The RMES is a lengthy questionnaire that reveals the testee's relational modality, that is, if one is dominant or submissive, if one communicates anger or holds it back, if one is more passive or more active in interpersonal relations. There are no right and wrong answers. All are equally valid and they are the accurate relational reflections about how the testee relates and how he/she will continue to relate throughout life.

**Transparent Mask Test (TMT)**

The second test leads to the creation of a sequence of masks. Masks cover up, but also reveal a person's feelings. The test encourages a person to become comfortable with being open as well as introspective.

**Balloon Portraits and Story (B P & S)**

The third test is about the testee's key social systems, his family of origin and marital family. The convention in this drawing is to present the members of one's family as balloons. Balloons are simple to draw. This simplifies the demands on one's artistic capacities. The coloring and the display of the balloons illustrate well the magnetic field of one's formative years and of current realities. Parents and siblings, spouses and children are the magnets that shape one's fields of power and powerlessness forces, one's model conflicts and resolutions.

**Conflictual Memories Test (CMT)**

A conflictual memory from childhood is the subject of the next test. This memory is of great significance because it determines the area of sensitivities and of strengths(mastery pursuits) as a person applies him- or herself to rectify things during the rest of his/her life. The childhood conflict reveals one polarity of the individual's magnetic field.

**Metaphor Construction Tests (Animal Metaphor Test - Fairy Tale Metaphor - Short Story - Intensified Animal Metaphor Test)**

The next group of tests leads to the construction of metaphors. The contents of these metaphors reveal the individual's strivings for mastery. These strivings usually directly offset passivity experiences as identified in the tests of the masks, family balloons portrait, and memory of childhood conflict. This spontaneous occurrence is a demonstration of the equilibrial compensatory processes of the mind.

The metaphors pertain to the creation of two figures and of a dialogue between them. The choice of figures reflects the structure of the magnetic forces of one's mental force field . The conversation between these two figures reveals the pattern of energy flow of conflict generation and conflict resolution, of energetic intertransformation within the personal system. The metaphor minisystem reveals the personal macrosystem.

**Dream Analysis (DA)**

Next, a report of a dream gives supplementary insights about one's fears or wishes in the process of attaining mastery.

**House-Tree-Person and Scribble (HTP,Scr.)**

The battery is completed with two simple tests: the drawings of a house, a tree and a person, and finally of a scribble. These tests accompanied by a short story reveal issues that are of significance to the testee.

## Section #3: The Formal Role Analysis Process (FRAP)

Following the testing, the trainee reviews and interprets the information, sums up insights , and composes self-evaluation reports. The process of compilation of information is channeled through leading questions and processes finally formulated along the ten levels of the Formal Analysis Profile (FAP).

**Level 1:** we identify the key role behavior, its reciprocal (activity and passivity) and opposite (cooperative and antagonistic) forms. These define the testee's structural space, the dimensions of his/her symbolic universe.

**Level 2**: we place the metaphor characters in the symbolic universe recognized at Level 1. Within the system each entity has now specific reference dimensions along the variables of social status, activity and passivity, and emotional quality.

**Level 3** we identify the intensity of conflict by recognizing the extent of the disturbance of dependency needs.

**Level 4** we uncover the energetic modalities present in the system and the quality of the flow of the energetic intertransformations necessary for the processing of conflict toward resolution.

**Level 5** we identify the areas of conflict where energy is blocked, polarized, or fixated.

**Level 6** we identify the generation and resolution of conflict, that is, the dialectic nature of relational patterns.

**Level 7** we graphically present both interpersonal dynamics and the syndromal patterns of the person

**Level 8** we identify the testee's relational modality, that is, the direction of one's movement in the power field given the alternatives of subordinacy/ dominance, cooperation/antagonism.

**Level 9** we identify the intensity of the testee's relational modality and other variables derived from the testing.

**Level 10** we identify the testee's capacity to transform conflict energy into insight in order to deal effectively with reality.

## Section #4: Skills DeverlopmentRelational Pattern Modification or Formal Analysis Skills Training (FAST)

This final segment of the training is of paramount significance in order for a person to evolve past the recognition of a pattern into its modification. The process of growth hinges on the resolution of old patterns and the acceptance of new ones. The progression is one of energetic leaps from one attitude to another, from a certain dated sense of self, the related perceptual perspective and the related defensiveness, to a more effective social self-placement, related change of perceptions, and adjusted communications. The modification of a relational pattern coincides with acquiring improved communicational skills.

# THE THEORY:
# CONFLICT ANALYSIS LECTURE SERIES (CALS):
# UNDERSTANDING THE LANGUAGE OF METAPHORS

**LECTURE #1: Our Culture, the Reign of Uninterpreted Metaphors.**
**Content**: In traditional philosophical systems, i.e.: religions, political and psychological theories, the truth is identified in a paradigmatic model. These perspectives promote a model structure of authority relations as though it were of universal value. When statements of universal validity are made axiomatically, methodologically, this order of thinking is labeled propositional. Formal Theory's methodology is relational. In this methodology, what matters is the relation or form between elements of a system. According to the formal method, the universal truths, rules, or formulas in behavior are not predicated upon the veracity of the premises, but upon the structure or relation of the elements in the totality or universe.

A metaphor story is provided as a sample universe of discourse to illustrate the methodological alternatives. This drama is obviously a fiction, but its structure is shown to demonstrate a typical Conflict Resolution Process. It consists of a system of interrelated transformations of one theme departing from a conflict and leading to a compromise or a resolution.
**Recommended Readings:** Volume I; Preface: Fireflies, Introduction: Arthur Staats Article on Methodological Positivism, Chapter I: Methodology.

**LECTURE #2: The Greek Creation Metaphors Revealing the Secrets of the Mind. Conflict Resolution Process as the Atomistic Unit for the Analysis of Behavioral Phenomena.**
**Content:** A perfect metaphor system, the Greek cosmogony myths, exemplifies the formal structuring of a system of dramatic transformations. We identify this dramatic entity as the **Conflict Resolution Process (CRP)**. This process is repeated five times across the five generations of the Greek creation, thus it is shown to be the atomistic entity of behavioral phenomena. The Conflict Resolution is manifested in the cosmogony as an intergenerationally transmitted lifetime pattern, which led from the cosmic chaos of the primordial Greek family to the perfect civilization of Athens. Formally, the Conflict Resolution Process represents a dialectic organization of ideational and biopsychosocial transformations, which clinically amounts to a model syndromal entity.
**Recommended Readings:**Volume I; Chapter V - Cosmogony as a Model of Formal Analysis, Graves: Greek Myths, Levi-Strauss: Structuralism, Freud: Interpretation of Dreams.

**LECTURE #3: Rigorous Methodology for the Scientific Study of Conflict/Metaphors-The Formal Analysis Profile - Stemming from the Disciplines of Logic, Mathematics, and Physics.**
**Content:** The **Conflict Resolution Process** is ideationally a **logical form**, and mathematically a **group of transformations**; physically, it is an **oscillatory process of energetic intertransformations**. Therefore, **it is subject to analysis by the disciplines of logic, mathematics, and physics**. These disciplines are explored in depth and constructs and formulas are presented along the **ten levels of formal analysis: The Formal Analysis Profile**.
**Recommended Readings:** Volume I; Preface, Glossary - Columns 1 and 2, Chapter II: Assumptions, Chapter III: The Formal Analysis Profile, Sources on Logic, Mathematics, and Physics.

**LECTURE #4: The Physics of Conflict and of Metaphors: Formal Analysis of the Conflict Resolution Process.**

**Content:** Freud placed emphasis on conflict as energy. Levi-Strauss and Piaget focused on ideas as forms. The Formal Theory reconciles the two perspectives. **Scientific rigor in the study of behavior is demonstrated through the parallel analysis level by level, of a natural science phenomenon, the Simple Harmonic Motion (SHM), and a model behavioral phenomenon, that of the Conflict Resolution Process.** It is shown that pertinent information for the study of behavior lies in the logic of relations, the mathematics of group theory, and the physics of the Simple Harmonic Motion (SHM).

Accordingly, a process of intertransformations evolves from the unstable state of conflict to the stable state of resolution and growth (Level 6); the Conflict Resolution Process is a system of formally related ideas(Level 1), which have physical dimensions(Level 2), and which consist of energy(Level 3). This energy is conserved(Level 4). Forces of conflict are opposite to the displacement from the rest state(Level 5). The process has a diagrammatic representation(Level 7). It is characterized by directedness(Level 8), quantification(Level 9), and qualification(Level 10).

**Recommended Readings:** Preface, Glossary and Chapter III - The Formal Analysis Profile.

**LECTURE #5: The Formal Spectrum of Alternative Moral Imperatives. Cross Cultural Normative Variations of the Conflict Resolution Process.**

**Content:**The Conflict Resolution Processes of the Greek, the Judaic, the Oriental, and the Mexican Indian cultures are contrasted as to the structuring of interpersonal relations. They are shown to be formally related to each other as opposite and reciprocal alternative forms. In each culture, the particular structuring of relations is pervasive throughout all interpersonal systems. The particular structuring is equally evident in cosmogony stories, political order, religious metaphors, educational philosophies, family relations, athletic games, musical compositions, and animal metaphors of the respective culture. Analysis of the systems yields consistently the cultures' distinct ways of structuring authority relations.

**Recommended Readings:**Preface, Dedication pages, Chapters V: Greek Cosmogony, Chapter VI: Personality Development, Chapter X: Ethics-Politics-Health, Textbooks on Anthropology.

**LECTURE #6: Formal Analysis of the Creative Process: Analysis of the Logic of the Metaphorical Language in Dreams, Dramas, Musical Compositions, and the Visual Arts; Two Exemplary Studies: Freud's Irma's Dream and The Gorski Retrospective.**

**Contents:**Comprehensive formal analysis of conscious and unconscious mental productions confirms the universality of the formal organization of associations. Aristotle described in "Poetics" this organization to characterize dramatic plays. Ibsen actualized it in his plays, Freud articulated it in his dreams, and artist Gorski manifested it in his canvases. The retrospective study of Gorski's work demonstrates three principles of formal organization of ideas. 1. The canvases evolve as formal transformations of a key theme, 2. they evolve as multiple consecutive sequences of conflict resolution processes, and 3. these sequences represent an ongoing maturational identity formation process.

**Recommended Readings:** Volume I; Preface: FAP of Gorski paintings, Volume I;Chapter IV: Formal Analysis of Behavior, Volume II: The Study of the Dreaming Process, Volume VIII: The Gorski Retrospective: From Art to Science.

**Continued on Page 7**

# THE FORMAL ANALYSIS PROFILE

## Ten Levels for the Reduction of Psychosocial Phenomena
## Ten Laws Determining Order in the Symbolic Universe

### LEVEL 1: FORMAL ANALYSIS: LAWS OF MATHEMATICAL GROUPS

Law of Inverse: Opposite States:
Cooperation-Antagonism $a + (-a) = 0$
Reciprocal States:
Activity-Passivity $a \cdot 1/a = 1$

The elements of an ideational universe are formally related as determined by the laws of mathematical groups: closure, associativity, identity, inverse. Accordingly, the totality of an individual's ideas are formally related to each other, they constitute the person's ideational or symbolic universe and obey, i.e., the law of inverse: Inversely related states are either opposite (cooperative versus antagonistic) or reciprocal (passive versus active) to each other.

### LEVEL 2: VARIABLES OR CONSTRUCTS ANALYSIS:

Displacement-S=Social Status
Acceleration-a=Motivational Force
Velocity-v=Behaviors
Mass-m=Investment
Mutual Distance-l= Alienation

The elemental unit of a symbolic system constitutes a binary distinction or conflict which has measureable dimensions. Thus any conflict as a particular binary distinction corresponds to a clearly identifiable position in the conflict's continuum defined as a formal symbolic universe. This position may be determined according to a number of measurable behavioral variables equivalent to those encountered in the study of the Simple Harmonic Motion (SHM), social status shift (displacement), behaviors (velocity), feelings (acceleration), involvement (mass), energy, etc.

### LEVEL 3: ENERGETIC INDUCTION ANALYSIS:

Conflict=Energy, $E = F \cdot S = (m_1 m_2 / l^2) \cdot S$

Conflicts are energetic quantities whose intensity is determined as the product of the subject's dependency needs times this individual's displacement from his/her equilibrial or rest position.

### LEVEL 4: ENERGETIC CONSERVATION OR ENERGETIC INTERTRANSFORMATION ANALYSIS:

$$E_{total} = E_{dynamic} + E_{kinetic} + E_{momentum} = E_{psychic} + E_{social} + E_{biological}$$

In behavior, as well as in physics, energy is conserved under the circumstances of closure.. We recognize in behavior several types of energy parallel to those in physics. The psychic, social and biological energetic modalities, are seen as equivalent to physics' dynamic, kinetic and momentum energy types. Among the three modalities, we distinguish qualitatively those that are labile, which tend to decompose themselves, and those that are stable. Labile psychic energy is gradually transformed into stable social energy. Conflicts in behavior undergo an ongoing process of oscillatory intertransformation through the three modalities of energy. Contrary to what is happening in physics, where entropy is raised, this process leads in the domain of beings to the progressive loss of entropy (psychic tension energy) and the increase of endelechy (meaning conformity energy, synergy or harmony). The oscillatory process continues ad infinitum until all unstable forms of energy are converted into stable energetic forms (psychic energy is transformed into psychosocial harmony).

## LEVEL 5: CONFLICT ANALYSIS:

| Conflict Force $a = -1/2\, K \bullet S$ |
|---|

In conflicts the motivational force(a) is proportional and opposite to the social status shift (displacement-S) of the individual from the rest state. Conflicts (forces) vary accordingly with the need realm (displacement) of the equilibrial disturbance. The rest state or state of zero distinctions corresponds to the individual's zero need, satiation, or equilibrial state.

## LEVEL 6: CONFLICT RESOLUTION OR SYNDROMAL ANALYSIS:

| $S = A \sin \theta$, $a = -a_c \sin \theta$, $v = v_c \cos \theta$ |
|---|

The conflict resolution process, the six-role dialectic pattern, is an energy transformational pump. It transforms labile psychic energy into stable energy social-personal order. The six-role process consists of orderly and predictable, periodically reproducible energetic transformations, mathematically definable as trigonometric functions of the three oscillating variables: status-S, motivational forces-a, and related behaviors-v. Clinically these cyclic energetic intertransformations correspond to the syndromal sequencing of behaviors.

## LEVEL 7: GRAPHIC ANALYSIS:

| Structural and Longitudinal Drawings |
|---|

Conflict states and processes may be portrayed graphically. The structural portrayal consists of vectorial depiction of social displacements and emotional forces on the reference circle. The longitudinal portrayal consists of sinusoidal curves depicting the trigonometric variations of interrelated variables (S,a,v)as function of time.

## LEVEL 8: RELATIONAL MODALITY ANALYSIS

| Distinct Syndromal Entities: Dominance versus Subordinancy |
|---|

We distinguish four alternative relational syndromally distinct modalities. The four alternative relational modalities are: subordinacy, cooperative and antagonistic; dominance, cooperative and antagonistic.

## LEVEL 9: QUANTITATIVE ANALYSIS I.E. MEASUREMENT OF BEHAVIORAL PARAMETERS THROUGH THE CONFLICT ANALYSIS BATTERY :

| CAB: RMES, Masks, Balloons, Conflict, Metaphor Tests, F.R.A.P. |
|---|

States of conflict may be qualitatively and quantitatively determined. This may be achieved through the formal analysis of uniformly generated personal symbolic systems. i.e., as elicited through the standardized metaphor tests of the Conflict Analysis Battery.

## LEVEL 10: HEALTH -EFFICIENCY ANALYSIS:

| Effectiveness=Efficiency=n = $E_{useful} / E_{total}$ |
|---|

The index of effectiveness or health consists in the individual's capacity to utilize his/her energetic resources, i.e., convert conflict energy into meaning (personal insight and social order, endelechy energy). This may be determined by the amount of insight derived (useful energy) from a standard test task, the standardized total energy expended.

# GLOSSARY OF THE FORMAL THEORY BASED ON THE ANNOTATED FORMAL ANALYSIS PROFILE (FAP)

Comparative Presentation of the Ten Levels of Abstraction-Reduction of a Natural and a Social Science Phenomena

| Level | Pure Science Discipline | Natural Science Phenomenon | Social Science Phenomenon |
|---|---|---|---|
| | Methodology<br>Logic<br>Mathematics<br>Physics<br>Trigonometry<br>Ethics | Simple Harmonic Motion (SHM)<br>The simple back and forth oscillation of a pendulum | Conflict Resolution Process (CRP)<br>The periodic repetition of a three-cycle, six-role sequence of transactions occurring in each of the five generations of the Greek cosmogony: Role Oppression-RO, Role Assumption-RA, Anticipated Role Reversal-ARR, Counterphobic Role Assumption-CPRA Role Reversal-RR,Compromise Role Assumption-CRA |

ROLE: Murdering

RO - Role Oppression - Threatened to be murdered
RA - Role Assumption - Murdering Parent
ARR - Anticipation of Role Reversal - Anticipating to be murdered
CPRA - Counterphobic Role Assumption - Murdering one's children
RR - Role Reversal - Being murdered by one's children
CRA - Compromise Role Assumption - Cursing one's children to be murdered

**Level 1 Formal Analysis**

Logic: Laws of relational logic

Group theory of mathematics: Law of Inverse:

In every mathematical group, for every element, there is an inverse element, which, combined with the first, yields the identity element

Under the operation of addition, the inverse elements are opposite
a + (-a) = 0

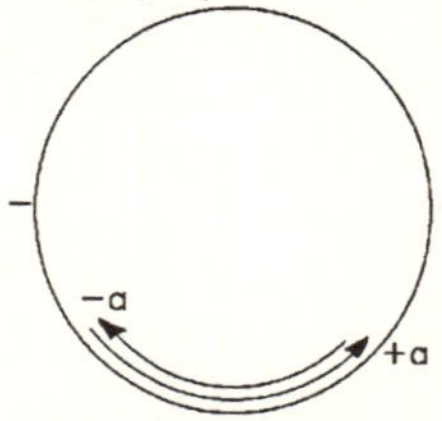


Inverse constructs:
Opposites are the clockwise vs. the counterclockwise rotation

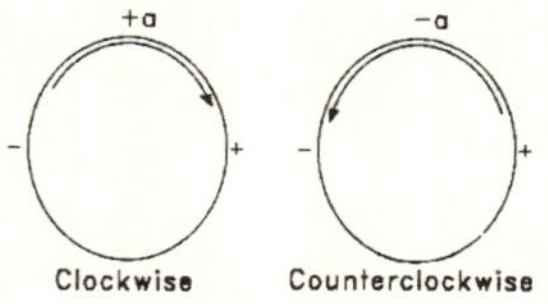


Opposite constructs: cooperative (marked as positive) vs. antagonistic (marked as negative)

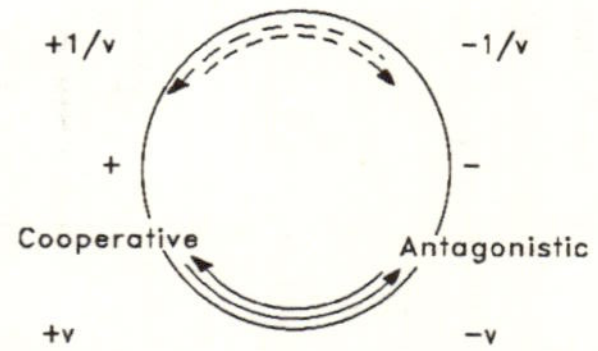


Under the operation of multiplication the inverse elements are reciprocal
a • 1/a = 1

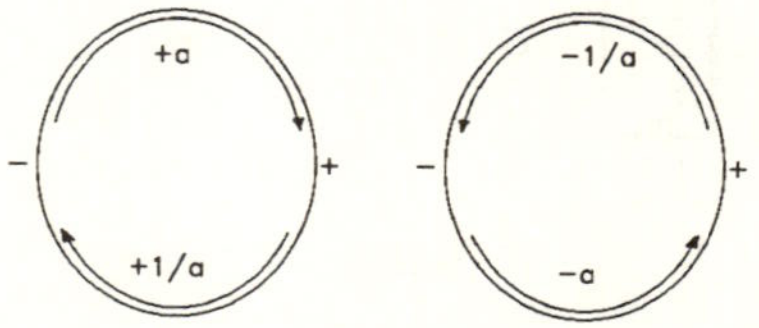


Reciprocals are the two same directional rotations distinguished as the passive and the active alternatives

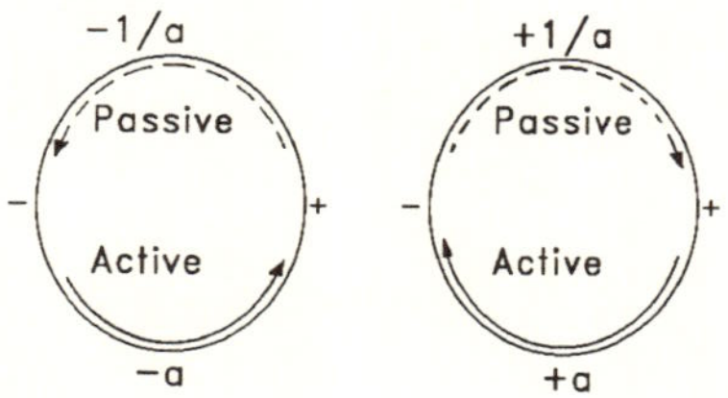


Reciprocal constructs:Direction for the scoring of antagonism (-) vs. cooperation (+) passivity (1/S) vs. activity (S)

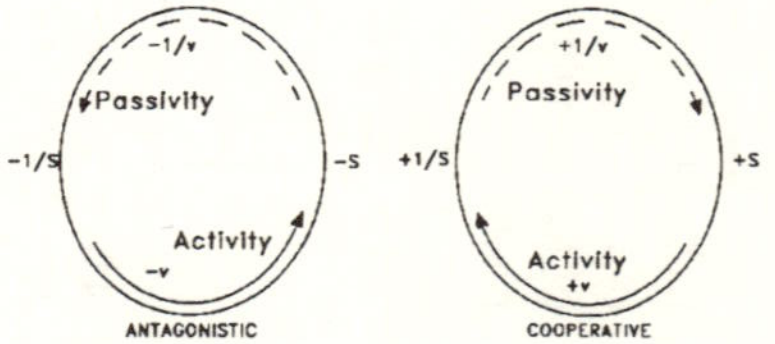

| Level | Pure Science Discipline | Natural Science Phenomenon | Social Science Phenomenon |
| --- | --- | --- | --- |
| Level 2<br>Variables<br>Analysis | Physics<br>Variables of the SHM<br>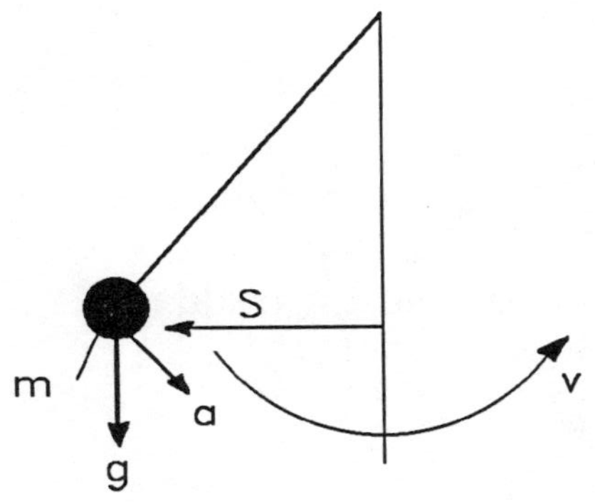<br> | The Simple Harmonic Motion is conceptualized as a function of the following symbolically identified variables:<br>Displacement= S<br>Maximum displacement=A (amplitude of the oscillation)<br>Velocity=v<br><br>Acceleration=a<br><br>Force= F gravity = g<br>Mass= m<br>Energy= E | The 6-role sequence is conceptualized as a function of the following behavioral variables equivalent to physics:<br>Normative Deviation= Status Differential= S<br>(-S status of aggression; -1/S status of being a victim of aggression)<br>Social conduct =v<br>(-v murdering<br>-1/v being murdered)<br>Motivational Force= a<br>(-a wishing to murder;<br>-1/a fear of being murdered)<br>Dependency Needs=g<br>Involvement = m<br>Conflict = Energy = E |
| Level 3<br>Energetic<br>Induction<br>Analysis | Physics<br>Lenz's Law<br>Principle of induction of energy | The energy of an oscillating pendulum is equal to the product of the ball's gravity (weight) times the ball's displacement from the position of equilibrium. | The energy of a harmonically evolving person is equal to the product of his/her dependency needs and displacement from the point of rest. |
| | $E = F \cdot S = (m_1 m_2 / r^2) \cdot S$ | *Energy= Force • Displacement* | *Conflict= Dependency Needs•Normative Deviation* |
| Level 4<br>Energetic<br>Conservation<br>Analysis | Physics<br>Law of the conservation of energy: Energy can neither be created nor destroyed, only transformed | The energy of an oscillating pendulum is constant and equal to the sum of the kinetic ($E_{kin}$), the potential ($E_{pot}$) and momentum ($E_{mom}$) energies as registered at any given instant.<br>The sum ideally is equal to the initial energy imparted to the system($E_{tot}$). | For any individual in conflict at every instant the sum of social energies (action and speech), psychic energies (feelings and thoughts), and biological energies (drives and impulses) is constant and equal to the energy imparted to the individual upon inception of the conflict. |
| | $E_{tot} = E_1 + E_2 + E_3$ | $E_{total} = E_{kinetic} + E_{potential} + E_{momentum}$ | $E_{total} = E_{social} + E_{psychic} + E_{biological}$ |

| Level | Pure Science Discipline | Natural Science Phenomenon | Social Science Phenomenon |
|---|---|---|---|
| Level 5 Conflict or Motivational Analysis | Physics | SHM is the type of vibratory motion in which the acceleration, a, is proportional and opposite to the displacement, S. Acceleration, a, is always directed towards the rest position. | Conflict Resolution Process is the type of periodic occurrence in which the emotional motivational driving force, a, is proportional to the normative deviation and always directed toward the rest state. |
| | $F = a =- 1/2KS =-KS$ | *Acceleration= -K•displacement* | *Motivational Force=-K• Normative Deviation* |
| Level 6 Syndromal Analysis | Trigonometry | The displacement S, velocity v, and acceleration a, are phase related trigonometric functions | The behavioral totality is a syndrom whose variables, S, v, a, are correlated asthe following trigonometric functions |
| | $S = A \sin\theta$<br>$a = -a_C \sin\theta$<br>$v = v_C \cos\theta$ | *Displacement =Function+ sin θ*<br>*Acceleration =Function - sin θ*<br>*Velocity =Function cos θ* | *Normative Deviations are a Function + sin θ*<br>*Emotions are a Function - sin θ*<br>*Behaviors are a Function cos θ* |

Level 7 Graphic Analysis

Graphic illustration of trigonometric variables as function of time:

Structural Diagram

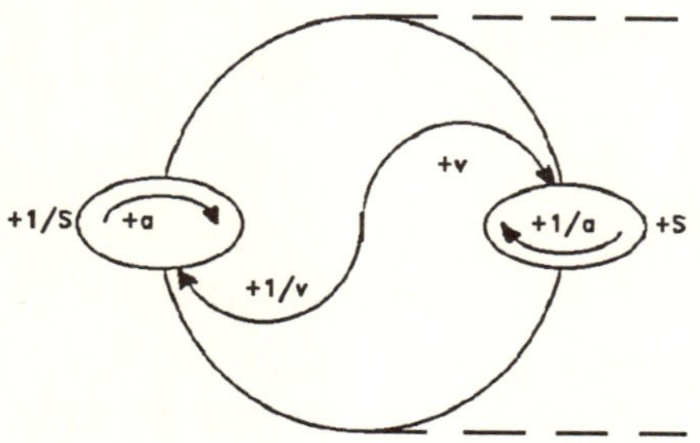


Longitudinal Diagram

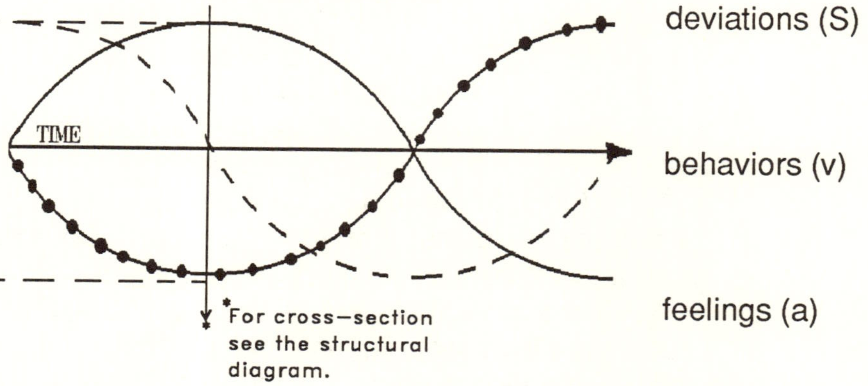

| Level | Pure Science Discipline | Natural Science Phenomenon | Social Science Phenomenon |
| --- | --- | --- | --- |
| Level 8<br>Relational<br>Modality<br>Analysis | Physics<br>Direction of a disturbance within the equilibrial space identified by the 4 inverse alternatives, relational or cardinal references<br>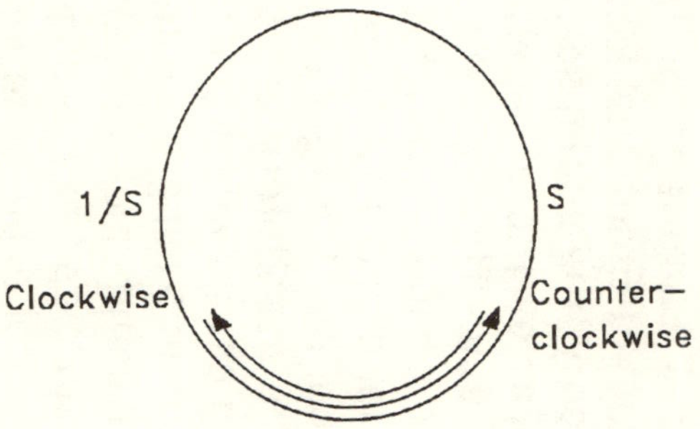 | 1. Direction of circular velocity, w<br>2. Direction of the oscillation toward a pole of the field<br>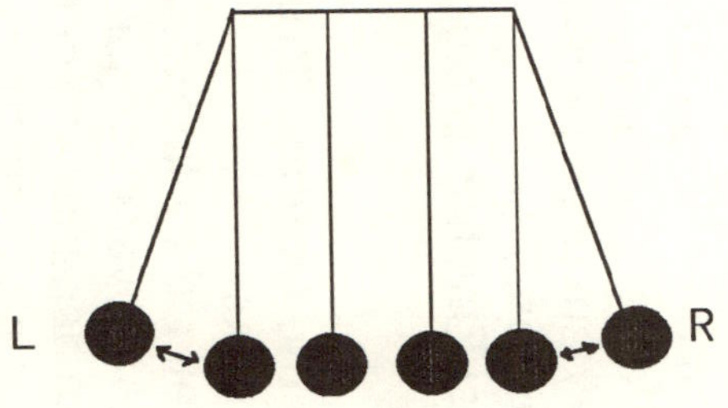<br>Range of motion in a system of pendulums | 1. Direction of circular velocity cooperation (clockwise) vs. antagonism (counterclockwise)<br>2. Direction toward pole of dominance or subordinancy.<br>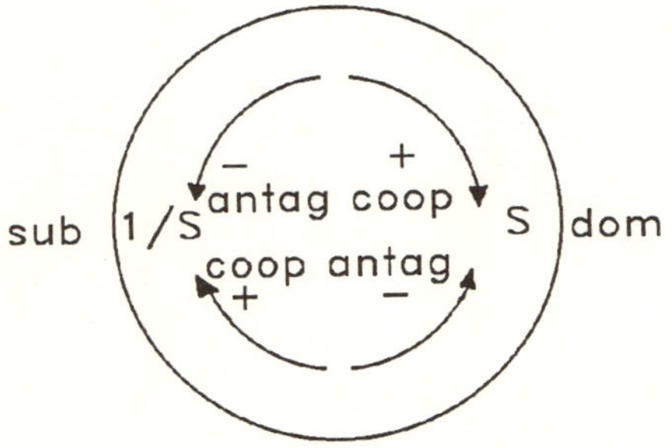 |
| Level 9<br>Quantitative<br>Analysis | The measurement of variables through the use of standardized units of measurement<br><br>*Standardized units of reference* | Quantitative determination of the variables through the use of metric measuring units<br><br>*i.e., the metric system* | Determination of variables through standardized projective and inventory psychological instruments,<br><br>*i.e., normative systems calibrated through the Conflict Analysis Battery.* |
| Level 10<br>Efficiency<br>Health or<br>Ethical<br>Analysis | Physics:<br>n= work useful/work provided<br>Efficiency is equal to the fraction of useful work over total work provided to a system<br><br>*n=* $E_{useful} / E_{total}$ | $n \to 1$ Motion finite: Friction $\to 0$<br>$n \leq 1$ Motion short lived: Friction high<br>$n = 1$ Perpetual motion Friction = 0<br>Efficiency determines the usefulness of a machine as a transformer of energy<br><br>*Efficiency=* $E_{useful} / E_{total}$ | $n \to 1$ Friction↓ coop↑ conflict↓<br>$n \to 0$ Friction↑ antag↑ conflict↑<br>Effectiveness is defined as the individual capacity to transform stress into insight.<br>Health is defined as the optimal structuring of relationships to maximize effectiveness.<br><br>*Effectiveness=* $E_{insight} / E_{stress}$ |

Continued From Page 6

**LECTURE #7: Personal Insights Through Metaphor Construction and Analysis: The Conflict Analysis Battery (CAB)- Formal Psychodiagnostic Testing for Measuring the Individual Conflict Resolution Process.**

**Contents:**Toward evaluation of the individual for diagnostic and therapeutic purposes, we elicit the systematic creation of metaphors, which may be thoroughly analyzed along the ten levels of the Formal Analysis Profile. Aspects of the Conflict Resolution Process sequence are addressed by particular testing instruments: Role Oppression is identified through the **Conflictual Memories and the Balloon Tests.** Role Assumption-Anticipated Role Reversal-Counterphobic Role Assumption dynamics are detected through the **Metaphor Tests.** Role Reversal - through the **Dream Analysis Test.** Role Reversal-Compromise Role Assumption - through the **Short Story Metaphor Test.**The reversed role sequence is reflected in the **Transparent Mask Test.**The Role Assumption-Anticipated Role Reversal relational choice is reflected through the **Relational Modality Evaluation Scale.**

**Recommended Readings:** Volume I, Chapter VIII: Formal Psychodiagnosis, Appendix: Validation Studies, Volume III: The Conflict Analysis Training.

**LECTURE #8: The Logic of Mental Illness as Metaphors Out of Control.**

**Contents:**Psychopathology is considered in terms of the spectrum of relational syndromal alternatives, along the four Relational Modalities and the range of quantitative and qualitative psychic tension variations: personality disorders, neuroses, and psychoses. Case studies illustrated by the Conflict Analysis Battery are used to demonstrate the nature of syndromal pathology and of psychic tension variations.

**Recommended Readings:**Chapters VII: Formal Psychopathology, IX: Psychotherapy, Appendix: Case Studies.

**LECTURE #9: Health, Ethics, and Politics as the Optimal Structuring of Relations. A Cross Cultural Study of Philosophical Outlooks.**

**Contents:** Relational optimalism as health is defined by formal or structural principles: communication as role reversibility, cooperation over antagonism, moderation over polarization, moderated dependence over intense dependence or intense independence, positive over negative attitudes. Cross-cultural studies confirm the universality of norms of moderation and concern for reciprocal relations.

**Recommended Readings:** Volume I; Chapter X: Ethics-Politics-Health.

**LECTURE #10: Understanding the Formal Language of Metaphors; Conflict Analysis Training: A Comprehensive Program of Emotional Education.**

**Contents:** **Because, through the Formal Theory, the social sciences have acquired the lucidity of the pure and natural sciences, a new moral imperative arises, the possibility and the necessity for emotional literacy.** The population has the civil right to be informed about problematic attitudes and about counterproductive parental and cultural Conflict Resolution Processes. Toward healthier or more effective communications with others, family, peers, and friends, the individual has the right to be informed. Hence, **programs of emotional education should be mandatory** and the school curriculum should include yearly Conflict Analysis Training or equivalent programs, i.e., lectures on the formal structuring of relations, self-assessment testing to accrue personal insight in one's own relational patterns, and interpersonal communicational skills exercises.

The content of the training is just as important as the message implicitly conveyed through its delivery. The delivery entails a model experience in fairness through the moderation of power on the part of the trainer, and implicit reinforcement of communicativeness, creativity, and assumption of responsibility on the part of the trainee.

**Recommended Readings:** Volume I: Chapter VIII: Formal Diagnosis, Volume III: Conflict Analysis Training, a Program of Emotional Education.

CONFLICT ANALYSIS TRAINING

FACT SHEET

DEMOGRAPHIC DATA

Date:______________________

Name:______________________________

Social Security #______________________

Address:

Number ___________Street___________

City __________________________

State ______Zip Code___________

Telephone: Home____________________

Work____________________

**FAMILY:**

Single_____ Married_____

Separated____ Divorced_____

Widowed_____ Remarried______

Number of children:_____________

Ages of children:_______________

Referred by:___________________

**SELF:**

Age:___Birthdate:_______________________

Religion:____________________________

Ethnic Origin:_________________________

Occupation:__________________________

Employer:____________________________

Address:

Number ________Street ______________

City ________ State____ Zip Code _______

**SPOUSE:**

Name:_________________________

Age:___Birthdate:_____________

Religion:____________________

Ethnic Origin:_______________

Occupation:__________________

Employer:____________________

Address:

Number________Street_____________

City_________State____Zip_________

**OBJECTIVE OF THE EVALUATION**

Psychotherapy_____

Emotional Education Training Program_____

Preemployment Screening_____

**RECENT PHOTOGRAPH**

**FEE STRUCTURE AGREEMENT:**

Fee per hour _______

Fee for total evaluation _______

Fee for training program_______

Medical Insurance Carrier______

Carriers terms for Psychotherapy services_____

Sponsor organization paying your training fees__________

## Note to the Trainee.

In the following section of the workbook, we have chosen to include more educational information for the trainee by inserting two studies:

1. An article summarizing the Formal Theory: **CONFLICT ANALYSIS - THE FORMAL THEORY OF BEHAVIOR INTRODUCES SCIENTIFIC CONCEPTUALIZATION IN THE STUDY OF BEHAVIOR** pp. 9a-19a

2. A demonstration of the Formal Theoretical analytical process on a complex case: **THE GORSKI RETROSPECTIVE PROVIDES EVIDENCE FOR THE SCIENTIFIC BREAKTHROUGH OF THE RECONCILIATION OF THE SOCIAL AND NATURAL SCIENCES** pp. 65-78

We hope the additional information inserted on the reverse side of the Conflict Analysis Battery and the Formal Role Analysis Profile will not interfere with your testing experience. On the contrary, we hope that this supplementary information will enhance it by clarifying the concepts and by illustrating their implementation in the analysis of metaphors.

**REASON FOR CONSULTATION** (Use back of paper for additional comments)

Check those problem areas which pertain to you:

Family___ Marital___ Occupational/Educational___ Crisis___ Personal Loss___
Phobia___ Obsession___ Compulsion___ Transgressiveness___
Anxiety___ Depression___ Hostility___ Anger___Guilt___ Shame___
Sleep Disorder___ Major Psychiatric Disorder___Drug Habit___
Smoking___ Alcohol Abuse___ Gambling___Legal Problems___
Eating Disorder___Sexual Disorder___Other Problem Areas___

Please describe problem areas:______________________________________________

____________________________________________________________________

____________________________________________________________________

Date of onset of problem:__________________________________________________

How is your life affected by your problem?___________________________________

____________________________________________________________________

____________________________________________________________________

What are your expectations from this consultation?_____________________________

____________________________________________________________________

____________________________________________________________________

**PSYCHIATRIC HISTORY**

Previous psychotherapy: Name(s) of therapist(s):_______________________________
Length of therapy, approximate dates:_______________________________________
Reason for past therapy:___________________________________________________
Hospitalization: Name of Hospital:____________________Date:________________

**MEDICAL HISTORY**

Name and address of private physician:______________________________________
Physical illnesses and allergies:____________________________________________

____________________________________________________________________

Medications (prescription and non-prescription) you are currently taking and amounts:___________________________________________________________

____________________________________________________________________

Medications you are allergic to:_____________________________________________
Alcohol intake, frequency and amount:_______________________________________

# CONFLICT ANALYSIS - THE FORMAL THEORY OF BEHAVIOR INTRODUCES SCIENTIFIC CONCEPTUALIZATION IN THE STUDY OF BEHAVIOR

**Conflict Analysis - The Formal Theory of Behavior** introduces a fundamental conceptual breakthrough, accomplishing the definitive upgrading of the study of behavior into the pure and natural science of conflict. This volume has been acknowledged by authorities as promising to become a classic for bridging the soft and the hard sciences. Leading psychologist Professor Donald Mosher of the University of Connecticut characterized the Formal Theory and its diagnostic testing as the "state-of-the-art in the state-of-the-science" conceptualization of behavior.

The Formal Theory conceptually integrates mental processes and social transactions. Ideas, emotions, behaviors, and biological phenomena are redefined into part aspects of a formal and energetic continuum in which order abides by the laws of logic, mathematics, and physics. This conceptual perspective reconciles conflicted theoretical positions as complementary views into a cohesive body of formal knowledge. This theoretical integration has multiple applications in organizing our perceptions of reality, in making diagnoses, and in conducting therapy.

The basis of **Conflict Analysis - The Formal Theory of Behavior** is that all ideational phenomena and manifest behaviors may be reduced to dialectic but also energetic oscillatory units constituting a totality, a dramatic sequence identified as **Conflict Resolution Process (CRP)**. The Conflict Resolution Process is initiated with a conflict and is completed with a resolution. Reality consists of ongoing Conflict Resolution Process - dramatic units, which are both ideational formal structures and energetic entities. Ideational, emotional, behavioral, and biological phenomena are ideas with a charge. They are intertransformable energetic modalities. The Conflict Resolution Process is biologically determined, since it is witnessed in the physiology of dreaming as well as of alert thinking and creativity. The biology dictates the necessity of the transformation of conflict into identity formation - compromise or insight, growth, acculturation, and spirituality.

Any ideational or behavioral phenomenon is assessed in the context of its symbolic universe, in the context of the circumscribed totality that is designated as Conflict Resolution Process, e.g., a canvas or an art exercise is not seen in isolation from the other paintings of an artist or in the art work of a testee, but in the context of continuous transformations. The Conflict Resolution Process is an organic dialectic entity that may be observed to transpire in any exchange, e.g., a sparse dialogue between two imaginary figures (as this occurs in metaphor testing processes), in the course of a dream, or during a lifetime thematic evolution. The strength of the theory is that rigorous methodology from the fields of logic of relations, group theory of mathematics, and physics' Simple Harmonic Motion converge in conferring to the analysis of this ubiquitous behavioral unit the features of a totality. The behavioral entity aquires meaning, order, and organization that have never before been available in this scientific domain.

The formal theoretical position evolved from observations that a pattern recurred in the ancient Greek family which was indicative of formal order in the realm of human relations. This pattern's particular structuring of relations, the Conflict Resolution Process, characterized the five consecutive generations of the Greek cosmogony (Diagrams 1 and 2).

The cosmogony's life cycle sequences adequately accounted for both intrapsychic and intergenerational processes in terms of formally organized ideational role systems. Unlike psychoanalysis, which focused on the Oedipal period in terms of genetically determined dynamics, Conflict Analysis ad-

## BIOGRAPHICAL INFORMATION

Past experiences that might have contributed to your being conflicted:

Describe troubled relationships and areas of conflict:

Describe dreams and nightmares:

Educational background:

Accomplishments you are proud of:

Ambitions and goals:

# THE CONFLICT RESOLUTION PROCESS

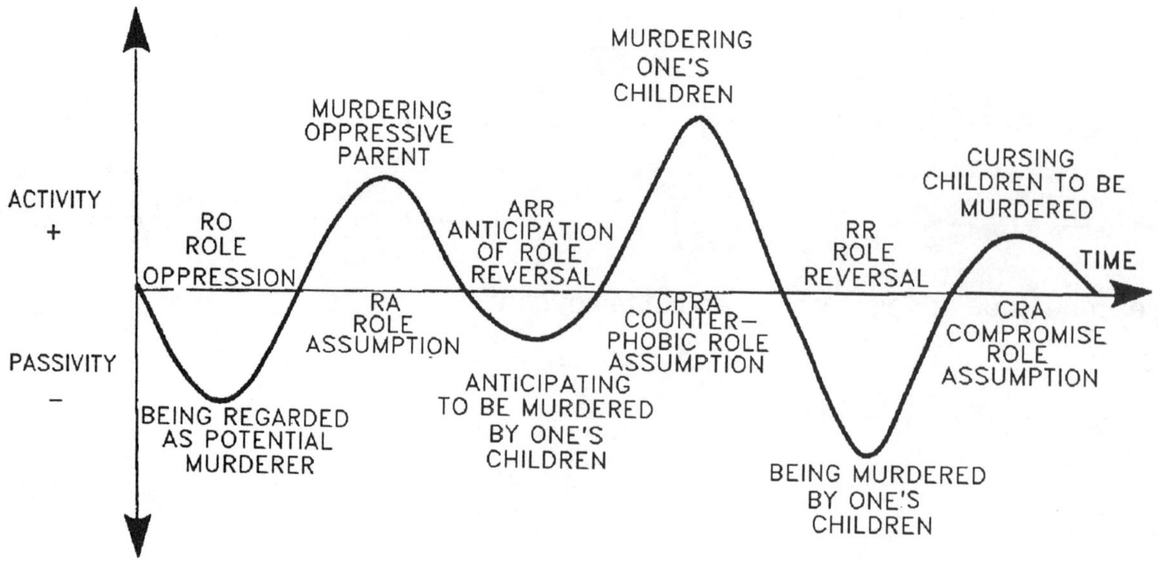


**Diagram 1:** The Oedipus myth, expanded by the formal analysis of the Greek cosmogony myths, has evolved into a key theoretical challenge for the Formal Theory: (1) It illustrates the formula of the dialectics of Ideational process. (2) It is the model of purely natural science processing of energetic disturbances. (3) The myth illustrates a particular kind of emotional, social structuring of relations, the dominance antagonism pattern prevelant in the Greek culture.

# THE MODEL OF THE GREEK CREATION MYTHS

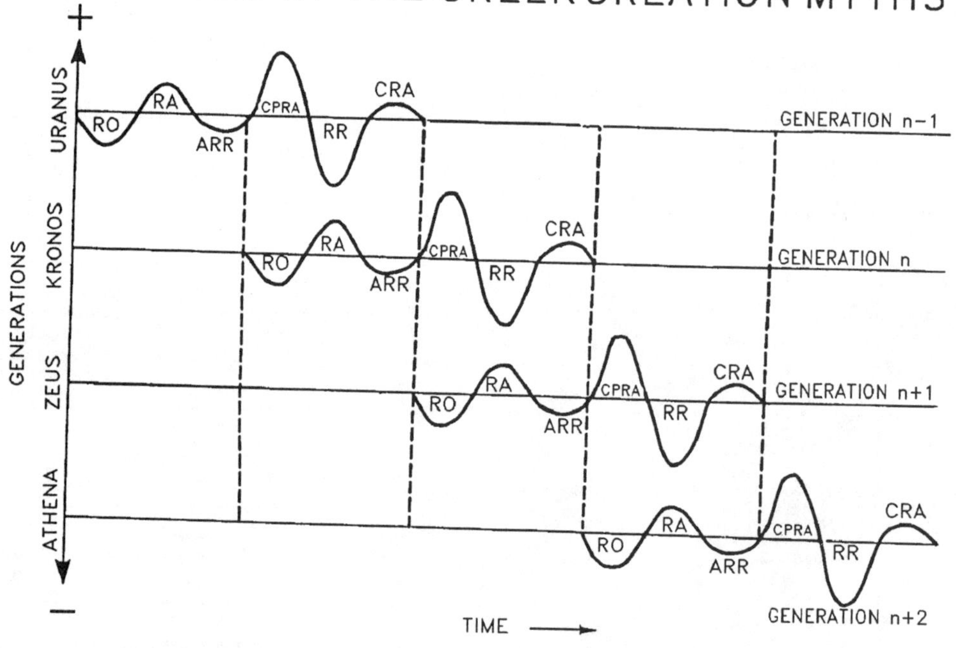


**Diagram 2:** The pattern repeats itself in 5 consecutive generations of the Greek cosmogonal family. We note that a lifetime sequence starts with the phase of role oppression. Fathers of the prior generation (generation *n-1*), afraid of being deposed by their children, murdered or oppressed them *(CPRA* generation *n-1* coincided with *RO* generation *n).* When the oppressed children of generation *n* came of age, they killed their father *(RA* generation *n* coincided with *RR* generation *n-1*). When the generation *n* children became fathers, they anticipated they would be killed by their own children *(ARR* generation *n).* Because of this fear, they counterphobically oppressed or murdered their children *(CPRA* generation *n* coincides with *RO* generation *n+1).* Eventually generation *n+1* grew of age and killed their fathers (generation *n* ). The life cycle ended when the generation *n* parent cursed his or her children to experience the same predicament, that the (generation *n+1*) in their turn be killed by their children, generation *n+2* (*CRA* generation n coinciding with *ARR* generation *n+1*).

## MEMBERS OF YOUR FAMILY

### PARENTS

Parents' marital status: Single__ Married__ Divorced__ Widowed__ Separated__ Remarried___

Father's name and age:____________

____________________

If deceased, date and cause of death:

____________________

Education:____________________

Occupation:____________________

Religion:____________________

Ethnic Origin:____________________

Mother's name and age____________

____________________

If deceased, date and cause of death:

____________________

Education:____________________

Occupation:____________________

Religion:____________________

Ethnic Origin:____________________

### BROTHERS AND SISTERS

Number of siblings:____________

Name:______________ Age:____

Name:______________ Age:____

Name:______________ Age:____

Name:______________ Age:____

Your birth order:____________

### SPOUSE

Name:__________________ Age:____

Indicate if you have been married before:

____________________

### CHILDREN

Name:__________________ Age:____

Name:__________________ Age:____

Name:__________________ Age:____

Name:__________________ Age:____

### HOME

Type of residence (house, apartment, condominium, etc.)____________________

Do you own your home?________

Who is presently living in your home?____________________

____________________

### IMPORTANT OTHERS

Best friend, name:__________________ Boss, name:____________________

Kinds of pets:____________________

### QUALITY OF RELATIONSHIPS

Circle the names of the above people to whom you are closest.

Underline the names of the people with whom you do not get along.

dresses ideational systems shaping reality of the entire lifetime and the continuum of intergenerational phenomena. For Conflict Analysis, ideational and social reality is a logical, predictable dialectic pattern of mental energetic intertransformations, which leads from a disturbance of equilibrium to a more stable new equilibrial state. The equilibrial disturbance evolves in terms of formally interrelated passivity/activity states, according to the Greek cosmogony: **Role Oppression**, a child is oppressed by his father. **Role Assumption**, the child aggresses against his father. **Anticipated Role Reversal**, the person anticipates to be hurt by his children. **Counterphobic Role Assumption**, he or she defensively eliminates them. **Role Reversal**, the outcome is the defensive person is indeed banished by one's children. **Compromise Role Assumption**, the resolution is that the deposed operator curses his or her children to the same fate that he or she suffered at the mercy of their own children.

The Conflict Resolution Process in the cosmogony myths leads to reduction of disorder and the increase of order, of integration, and of emotional growth and identity, that is, discovering meaning in spite of adjusting to restraints. Thus conflict resolution transforms conflict energy into insight, meaning or organization in the system of ideas, e.g., the Greek cosmogony's five generations organized the mental realities so that, at the end of its five generations, one notes a formidable acculturation. Instead of defensiveness and murder, we observe the attainment of an harmonious family system of loving and trusting relationships. Father Sky, Uranus, afraid of his children, killed his children from Mother Earth, Gaea, and was killed by his youngest son, Time, or Kronos. In his turn, the Titan, Kronos, afraid of his children, ate his Olympian infants as soon as Rhea, his wife, delivered them. Predictably, Kronos was killed by his son, Zeus. In his turn, Zeus afraid of his children, swallowed his wife Metis when she was pregnant with Athena; unlike previous generations, Athena, delivered from Zeus' head, respected her father, yet feared having a child and through a need for self preservation, chose to remain a virgin. Accidentally, a child was born from her, Erichthonius, who became the king of Athens and who appointed Athena as the patron goddess of Athens. The resolution of the cosmogony sequence of family power struggles departed from the initial cycle of primordial chaos, of violent infanticides and patricides, and led to the civilized Athenian culture with a consolidated religion, political and judicial systems, rules for athletic and dramatic games, and long lasting values which have influenced mankind.

The Formal Theory reconciles the Piagetian perspective of logical and mathematical operations with the Freudian dynamic clinical perspective concerned with energetic quantities. Conflict Analysis' "relations" are equivalent to Piagetian "forms" and Freud's "cathexes". But the relational unit for a formal analyst is not a mere form, or a mere energetic quantity. Formal relations are entities in constant transformation, like the oscillations of a pendulum; they have the elusive physical substance of intertransformable energetic charges. The Conflict Resolution Process as oscillations of the mind are characterized by intertransformations of behavioral energetic modalities equivalent to Simple Harmonic Motion's dynamic to kinetic and momentum modalities; in behavior we encounter during a Conflict Resolution Process cycle psychic energy, emotions, transformed into social energy or behaviors and into biological energy or impulses and vice versa. Thus the Simple Harmonic Motion surrenders to behavior's Conflict Resolution Process all its constructs and formulas. Behavior then becomes both a pure mathematical and a natural science, the exact science of conflict.

The CRP is a six-role sequence of associations which starts with a conflict and which is concluded with its resolution. It is an ideational process, a dialectic oscillatory phenomenon at each of ten levels of abstraction comparable to that of physics' Simple Hamonic Motion. The parallels between the two phenomena and the equivalent levels of abstraction, present in both realms, is identified as the **Formal Analysis Profile (FAP)**. Each level of analysis of the Formal Analysis Profile is characterized by a formula and pertains to

**CONFLICT ANALYSIS BATTERY**

**RELATIONAL MODALITY EVALUATION SCALE (RMES)**

Name:______________________
Date:______________Age:______

## Introduction and Instructions

This test helps you to identify both your relational modality, that is, your way of relating or communicating with others and the degree of psychic tension or intensity of conflict you currently experience. There are four major alternative categories of relating. These are the following: Submissive Cooperative, Submissive Antagonistic, Dominant Cooperative, Dominant Antagonistic. One is born with a relational modality or relational preference. Each relational modality has advantages and shortcomings, i.e., it is just as desirable to be dominant cooperative as submissive cooperative, submissive antagonistic as dominant antagonistic, etc. The psychic tension scores indicate areas and degree of conflict that you are experiencing. Elevations in these scales indicate that you may need to seek help or counseling.

The significance of relational modalities is that they determine the organization of personal and social reality for a person. The mechanism unerlying this organization is that relational modalities are structurally distinct conflict generation and conflict resolution patterns.

Clinically, we recognize organized and interconnected behavioral phenomena as syndromes. Syndromes are sequences of interrelated behaviors and emotions, e.g. a dominant individual opts for social power positions, fears powerlessness, relates defensively, is reduced to powerlessness, and finally reaches a compromise. It is important to identify one's relational syndromal modality because it is possible for particular repetitions of experiences in terms of circular self-fulfilling prophecy patterns.

This test consists of a questionnaire or inventory of items classified according to the four main syndromal categories. Under each syndromal category items are clustered according to a few common communicational and relational characteristics. Often the testee can instantly identify his or her relational modality simply by recognizing the scales and subscales along which he or she scores the strongest. Score the items by circling the number reflecting your degree of agreement or disagreement, strongly agree +3, moderately agree +2, mildly agree +1, mildly disagree -1, moderately disagree -2, strongly disagree -3. For example, you score the item "I expect too much of other people" according to how you relate by circling one of the following six choices:

I disagree:
strongly -3, moderately -2, mildly -1,

I agree:
mildly +1, moderately +2, strongly +3.

the domain of a correlation. **Level 1** addresses the analysis of a symbolic universe in terms of formally intertransformable role states. In **Level 2**, physics' constructs displacement (S), velocity (v), acceleration (a) find their equivalents in conflict science's social status (S), behaviors (v), and emotions (a). These constructs' trigonometric formulas account for the syndromal and oscillatory character of the Conflict Resolution Process studied under **Level 6**. The product of emotions (a) times status shift (S) becomes conflict energy (**Level 3**). The conservation of energy characteristic of the Simple Harmonic Motion is observed to characterize the Conflict Resolution Process and thus any conflict as an energetic system is seen to obey the principle of conservation. Emotions, behaviors, and biological states as energetic modalities in a system of conflict are seen as conserved. The intertransformation of states leads toward resolution, not as an entropic catabolic event, but as an anabolic mental transformation increasing order in the realm of ideas (**Level 4**). We may diagrammatically portray behavior. Diagrams are used to portray the structure of relations in any particular symbolic universe and also to portray emotions and behaviors (**Level 7**). (Diagram 3) The CRP is screened to diagnose relational modalities. In the context of the syndromal sequential structuring of relations, we distinguish dominant-subordinate and cooperative-antagonistic variations in the spectrum of alternatives.(**Level 8**). Effectiveness in solving conflicts entails optimal structuring of relations. Treatment recommendations are solicited to attain an attitude change, internal restructuring of relations, i.e., less dominance or subordinacy; less antagonism, more cooperation, and improved flow of communications (**Level 10**) (Table 1, Table 2 Glossary).

One may speculate that conflict resolution, or insight, amounts to the internalization of energy order or spirituality, inner meaning, or endelechy. While in the inorganic world, energy is broken down into entropy, the animal (especially the human) mind, with its conflict resolution capacity, like the plant world with the process of photosynthesis, captures and upgrades energy into emotional and social order or spiritual life. One may venture to say that the function of dramatic plays and musical compositions, as well as of dreams, consists of lowering disorder or conflict by imparting conflict resolution experiences; acculturation is experiencing harmony within a systemic orderly process. Catharsis and expiation may be easily reinterpreted along processes of conflict resolution as experiences in affirming identity formation or spiritualization.

Modified versions of the same Conflict Resolution Process are found in all cultural systems, e.g., the Judaic, Mexican Indian, and Oriental cosmogonies. These versions are formally related as opposite and reciprocal to each other. The Judaic and Greek cultures allocated to the individual a dominant position and supported the individual's dominating the collective and his seeking pleasure and immortality, the Judaic in a dominant cooperative mode, the Greek in a dominant antagonistic mode. By contrast, the Oriental and the Mexican Indian cultures define life as painful, indeed they prescribe that the individual suffer; individuality is subsumed to the collective and man is groomed to value pain and to endure it, even seek out death as freedom from the fate of being reborn. The ancient Mexican choice of subjecting man to life sacrifice corresponds formally to the submissive antagonistic conflict resolution, while the Oriental choice of total mastery of one's cravings, occasionally leading to self-sacrifice, represents the submissive cooperative alternative.(Diagrams 4 and 5) (Table 3 - Cultural Metaphors, Illustrations-Interpretations)

The structure of the four inversely related normative cultural environments may be observed by contrasting cultural metaphors pertaining to temptation. Formal analysis of cultural metaphors reveals each system's characteristic power structuring of relations. The apple metaphor symbolizes pleasure and informs on the relation of the individual versus the system. The fact that the Judaic creation regarded the apple as "forbidden," reflects that the culture is promoting moderation and cooperation. The fact that the Greek culture considered the apple as enviable, and symbolized it as an award-trophy for "the fairest" woman, reflects that

**DOMINANT COOPERATIVE SYNDROME**

| | Disagree | | | | | Agree |
|---|---|---|---|---|---|---|
| **Leadership** | | | | | | |
| 1. I demand that others cooperate with me | -3 | -2 | -1 | +1 | +2 | +3 |
| 2. If I think something is right I'll do it, no matter what the rules are | -3 | -2 | -1 | +1 | +2 | +3 |
| 3. I maintain my image at any cost | -3 | -2 | -1 | +1 | +2 | +3 |
| 4. I have always been a leader and enjoy it | -3 | -2 | -1 | +1 | +2 | +3 |
| 5. I like to tell others what to do | -3 | -2 | -1 | +1 | +2 | +3 |
| 6. I am usually the person who initiates and who takes charge of things in my relationships | -3 | -2 | -1 | +1 | +2 | +3 |
| 7. I make my needs known very clearly | -3 | -2 | -1 | +1 | +2 | +3 |
| 8. I feel other people would do a far better job under my supervision than on their own | -3 | -2 | -1 | +1 | +2 | +3 |
| Leadership Average Item Score | ______ | | | | | |
| **Competitiveness and Dominance** | | | | | | |
| 9. I get my way more often than I give in to others | -3 | -2 | -1 | +1 | +2 | +3 |
| 10. I am a dominant person | -3 | -2 | -1 | +1 | +2 | +3 |
| 11. I like to command power and authority over others | -3 | -2 | -1 | +1 | +2 | +3 |
| 12. I am very aware of how others dress, what they own and earn, where they live | -3 | -2 | -1 | +1 | +2 | +3 |
| 13. I have always been aware of who is ahead of me | -3 | -2 | -1 | +1 | +2 | +3 |
| 14. I have urges to do forbidden things | -3 | -2 | -1 | +1 | +2 | +3 |
| 15. I am boisterous and demonstrative | -3 | -2 | -1 | +1 | +2 | +3 |
| 16. I call attention to myself by speaking up a lot | -3 | -2 | -1 | +1 | +2 | +3 |
| 17. If I want to do something, I do it | -3 | -2 | -1 | +1 | +2 | +3 |
| 18. I have a comment all the time | -3 | -2 | -1 | +1 | +2 | +3 |
| 19. I'd like people to think I am the greatest. | -3 | -2 | -1 | +1 | +2 | +3 |
| Dominance Average Item Score | ______ | | | | | |
| **Personal Discomfort and Sensitivities** | | | | | | |
| 20. My problem is one of guilt | -3 | -2 | -1 | +1 | +2 | +3 |
| 21. I tend to feel patronized when somebody gives me a compliment | -3 | -2 | -1 | +1 | +2 | +3 |
| 22. I do not let others take advantage of me | -3 | -2 | -1 | +1 | +2 | +3 |
| 23. I am uncomfortable with the intensity of my cravings and impulses for food, sex, money, and need for attention. (Underline what is pertinent) | -3 | -2 | -1 | +1 | +2 | +3 |

## FORMAL THEORY'S CONCENTRIC CIRCLES MODEL

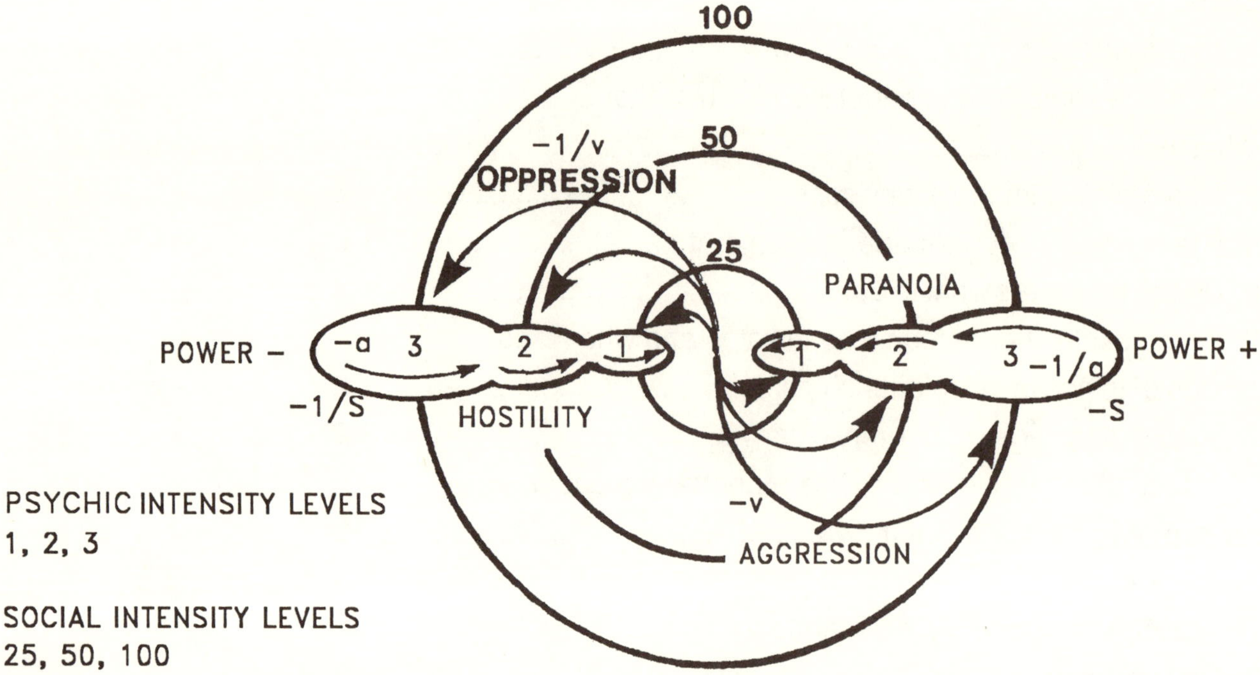


**Diagram 3:** Thus by using the key role relation to describe the three variables, those of norms, behaviores and feelings, any given system's complexity attains the conceptual simplicity of a natural phenomenon. Psychosocial Phenomena then may be analyzed along natural science variable correlations or formulas.

the Greek culture condoned antagonism and systemic polarization. Inversely, in the Mexican and Oriental cultures, man may expect pain, he is the sacrificial victim to the gods, man does not have power in the system. In Mexico, man, easily regarded as the desecrator of the status quo, is destined to be punished by life sacrifice. Man's disbelieving primordial mother wants his pulsating heart, man is the apple in her merciless hands. Alternatively, in the Orient, the apple is seen inflated in the image of the sacred cow and that man, even if he is starving, may not desire it. Indeed, man volunteers to sacrifice himself to combat the pain of his desires. These four cultures as formal alternatives are unified as four ways of defining correct relating for man. They are formally related as the opposites, cooperative versus antagonistic, and the reciprocals, dominant versus submissive relational alternatives.

To understand the Formal Theory and its implication for self-knowledge, a program has been devised, a program of emotional education. This is presented in a second publication identified as **Conflict Analysis Training (CAT)**. It consists of a series of lectures, the **Conflict Analysis Battery (CAB)**, a self-assessment psychodiagnostic test sequence, insight eliciting analyses of the testing, and finally communicational skills development exercises. The testing first elicits the creation of metaphors, art and text, and subsequently the systematic formal analysis of the metaphors, which leads to the development of self-assessment insights and also implicitly and explicitly, the demonstration of the theory.

Through formal analysis of metaphors we can measure the individual relational dimensions according to the ten levels of the Formal Analysis Profile. This approach constitutes a new psychodiagnostic technology. The Conflict Analysis Battery differs in three principal ways from traditional testing: (1) in terms of the target phenomenological entity, that it seeks to

| | Disagree | | | | Agree | |
|---|---|---|---|---|---|---|
| 24. I tell people who annoy me to leave me alone.................. | -3 | -2 | -1 | +1 | +2 | +3 |
| 25. I am easily frustrated when I don't get my way................. | -3 | -2 | -1 | +1 | +2 | +3 |
| 26. I do not like to depend on others.................................... | -3 | -2 | -1 | +1 | +2 | +3 |
| Discomfort Average Item Score | ______ | | | | | |
| **Defensiveness and Lack of Compassion** | | | | | | |
| 27. Depressed people wallow in self- pity. What they need is a good boot to jack themselves up............. | -3 | -2 | -1 | +1 | +2 | +3 |
| 28. I do not allow myself to cry in public................................ | -3 | -2 | -1 | +1 | +2 | +3 |
| 29. I expect too much of other people.................................. | -3 | -2 | -1 | +1 | +2 | +3 |
| 30. I don't let people know I have problems.......................... | -3 | -2 | -1 | +1 | +2 | +3 |
| 31. I can end relationships that are hurtful............................ | -3 | -2 | -1 | +1 | +2 | +3 |
| 32. I have difficulty accepting responsibility for the way I feel. | -3 | -2 | -1 | +1 | +2 | +3 |
| 33. I blame others when things do not work out..................... | -3 | -2 | -1 | +1 | +2 | +3 |
| Defensiveness Average Item Score | ______ | | | | | |

## DOMINANT ANTAGONISTIC SYNDROME

| | | | | | | |
|---|---|---|---|---|---|---|
| **Distrust** | | | | | | |
| 34. You are wise not to trust people...................................... | -3 | -2 | -1 | +1 | +2 | +3 |
| 35. Having to ask for help makes me feel like a failure........... | -3 | -2 | -1 | +1 | +2 | +3 |
| 36. I distrust being analyzed................................................ | -3 | -2 | -1 | +1 | +2 | +3 |
| Distrust Average Item Score | ______ | | | | | |
| **Provocativeness** | | | | | | |
| 37. I have a tendency to provoke people.............................. | -3 | -2 | -1 | +1 | +2 | +3 |
| 38. I attack people with little or no provocation...................... | -3 | -2 | -1 | +1 | +2 | +3 |
| 39. I do things to shock people............................................ | -3 | -2 | -1 | +1 | +2 | +3 |
| 40. I do some things regardless of others' feelings................ | -3 | -2 | -1 | +1 | +2 | +3 |
| Provocativeness Average Item Score | ______ | | | | | |
| **Dominance** | | | | | | |
| 41. I do not let anyone tell me what to do............................... | -3 | -2 | -1 | +1 | +2 | +3 |
| 42. I am a very bossy person................................................ | -3 | -2 | -1 | +1 | +2 | +3 |
| 43. I am a domineering person............................................ | -3 | -2 | -1 | +1 | +2 | +3 |
| Dominance Average Item Score | ______ | | | | | |
| **Intensity In Sensitivities and Responses** | | | | | | |
| 44. I either have enemies or loyal friends............................. | -3 | -2 | -1 | +1 | +2 | +3 |
| 45. If a person lets me down, I get infuriated and I let him/her know it.................................................... | -3 | -2 | -1 | +1 | +2 | +3 |

isolate for analytical purposes, (2) in terms of the analytical screening of information along the Formal Analysis Profile (FAP), (3) in the tester-testee contractual relationship.

(1) The CAB systematically explores the individual's symbolic universe in terms of units of the mini-phenomenon of analysis, the target sample dramatic process characteristic of the symbolic universe of the individual. The objective of formal diagnosis is to detect the order or structure of a symbolic universe, the system's key role and the process of its formal transformations toward an outcome. The object of formal psychodiagnosis, then, is not to identify isolated traits or states but to expose the formal syndromal integration of six sequential role relational states into a total dynamic or dramatic process, the individual's Conflict Resolution Process.

(2) The battery's elicited individual Conflict Resolution Processes are screened sytematically along the formal conceptual methodology's Formal Analysis Profile, a table of ten levels of abstraction- reduction of phenomenological reality.

(3) The CAB restructures the contractual relation between tester and testee. Each task addresses the recipient directly. The testee creates the art work and the text and gleans the insights. Furthermore, the service may be delivered by an educator in a group self-assessment emotional education program and may be self-administered. The process has many functions, e.g., it may be used for therapeutic ends. The Formal Theory's conceptual language and its CAB testing provide a means to discover insights about one's relational patterns and implicitly the recognition of areas that need improvement.

The personal testing record serves to demonstrate the theory through the formal analysis of the evolving symbolic universe of one creator's art work. The record illustrates clearly the Conflict Resolution Process in an exemplary thematic domain. In each of the testee's protocols, the progression of conflicts and insights obeys the principles of formal analysis: (1) The symbolic language consists in formally related transformations of a key theme. (2) The evolution in each exercise demonstrates the Conflict Resolution Process, and (3) the succession of resolutions illustrates the ongoing dialectic process of conflict resolution throughout a trainee's dramatic associations. This record documents the organization of ideas through internalization that promotes identity formation and spiritualization.

The Conflict Analysis Training is a comprehensive program of emotional education encompassing a series of lectures and the Conflict Analysis Battery testing. It expedites the process of psychotherapy for those in therapy and provides a course in accelerated development of insight for those who are not in therapy. Knowledge and insight are made available to the general public.

The Formal Theory has multiple applications in organizing our perception of reality. As such it introduces a new way of interpreting dreams, behavioral process, art, literature, drama and music based on the dialectic Conflict Resolution Process. Conflict resolution accounts for the self-healing function of creativity, which gradually leads to growth, that is, acculturation, and abstract philosophical thinking, that is of spirituality and science. The first volume is an extensive theoretical document that departs from the formal interpretation of myths, proceeds to the systematic formal analysis of individual metaphors, and leads to the present program of self-assessment.

The elusive goal of "know thyself" is finally clearly attainable. Behavior, which has been fragmented and conceptually unfocused as a domain of knowledge, is assured now the respectability of an exact science. A consequence of this discovery is that the public may have access to wisdom and morality bypassing the monopolies of ethical authority ministered by religious, political, and psychological organizations by relying more and more for ethical imperatives in the purely scientific study of the humanities.

| | | Disagree | | | Agree | |
|---|---|---|---|---|---|---|
| 46. I think I am better than anybody else | -3 | -2 | -1 | +1 | +2 | +3 |
| 47. I frequently talk louder than anyone else | -3 | -2 | -1 | +1 | +2 | +3 |
| 48. I hardly ever compromise. | -3 | -2 | -1 | +1 | +2 | +3 |
| 49. I am aloof | -3 | -2 | -1 | +1 | +2 | +3 |
| 50. I am stubborn | -3 | -2 | -1 | +1 | +2 | +3 |
| Sensitivities Average Item Score | ______ | | | | | |

**Explosiveness**

| | | | | | | |
|---|---|---|---|---|---|---|
| 51. My temper is short | -3 | -2 | -1 | +1 | +2 | +3 |
| 52. People barely have to annoy me and I explode | -3 | -2 | -1 | +1 | +2 | +3 |
| 53. I have difficulty holding my anger back | -3 | -2 | -1 | +1 | +2 | +3 |
| 54. My temper scares people off | -3 | -2 | -1 | +1 | +2 | +3 |
| 55. I occasionally get angry enough to want to kill | -3 | -2 | -1 | +1 | +2 | +3 |
| 56. I have fits of rage | -3 | -2 | -1 | +1 | +2 | +3 |
| 57. When criticized, I get mad and let people know it | -3 | -2 | -1 | +1 | +2 | +3 |
| Explosiveness Average Item Score | ______ | | | | | |

## DOMINANT ANTAGONISTIC EXTREMISM

**Established Oppositionality**

| | | | | | | |
|---|---|---|---|---|---|---|
| 58. I was always the black sheep of the family | -3 | -2 | -1 | +1 | +2 | +3 |
| 59. Whatever my parents wanted, as a child I did the opposite | -3 | -2 | -1 | +1 | +2 | +3 |
| Oppositionality Average Item Score | ______ | | | | | |

**Arrogance**

| | | | | | | |
|---|---|---|---|---|---|---|
| 60. I feel and act superior to others | -3 | -2 | -1 | +1 | +2 | +3 |
| 61. I am the kind of person who is right all the time | -3 | -2 | -1 | +1 | +2 | +3 |
| 62. I have a tendency to be sarcastic | -3 | -2 | -1 | +1 | +2 | +3 |
| Arrogance Average Item Score | ______ | | | | | |

**Provocativeness and Indifference to Others' Feelings**

| | | | | | | |
|---|---|---|---|---|---|---|
| 63. If I have a thought, however unpleasant to others, I say it loud and clear | -3 | -2 | -1 | +1 | +2 | +3 |
| 64. I tend to test limits, rules, and norms | -3 | -2 | -1 | +1 | +2 | +3 |
| 65. I tend to instigate arguments | -3 | -2 | -1 | +1 | +2 | +3 |
| 66. I pick on others | -3 | -2 | -1 | +1 | +2 | +3 |
| 67. In a discussion or argument, I have to have the last word... | -3 | -2 | -1 | +1 | +2 | +3 |

## AN EXERCISE OF FORMAL INTERPRETATION OF METAPHORS

The key distinction of cultures has been the ethical or normative regulation of man's power relationship with his fellow man as reflected in injunctions on how to deal with temptation or implicitly, desire for power. Normative injunctions have been conveyed intuitively through metaphors as well as explicitly through religious, political and philosophical articulations. It is opportune here to contrast the formal spectrum of moral alternatives of the four cultural perspectives mentioned above, and to accomplish this merely by contrasting formally equivalent metaphors regarding dealings with food. They all implicitly address normative issues of assuming power. Contrasting these cultural metaphors we may appreciate the simple clarity of formal language and demystify, or at least soften, the frightening, all encompassing moral imperatives of each cultural injunction.

The four cultural ethical alternatives to be considered may be reduced formally to dominant and submissive relating. Along the dominant modes, the Judaic is the dominant-cooperative (forbidden fruit), and the Greek is the dominant-antagonistic (apple of discord). Along the submissive modes, the Oriental is the submissive-cooperative (sacred cow), and the Mexican is the submissive-antagonistic alternative (the gods demand live human sacrifice).

In both dominant cultures, Judea and Greece, man saw the world as a place of pleasures, one in which he could satisfy his needs, in which he could prosper, master uncertainty and pursue immortality. In Judea, the condition for permanent happiness, that is immortality or paradise, was that the "apple", a symbol of temptation, be treated as forbidden, which entailed that in order for man to enjoy peace and power, he had to respect limits, hence the injunction of something being forbidden. Mosaic law confirmed the importance of cooperative behaviors by specifying the equivalent to the forbidden fruit as respect of another man's wife, property, authority and rights. By contrast, in Greece, the apple was defined as an enviable and desirable trophy. It was a glittering golden object inscribed by Ares(Eris), the god of war, "To the fairest". It was instrumental in the proliferation of strife which led to the Trojan War and to the inspiration of the great Homeric epics, and of a great number of Greek Tragedies. It metaphorically characterized the ubiquitous competitive Greek pattern of pursuing power, women, adventure, political, and athletic trophies. Hence, the Greek apple became known as the apple of discord.

Inversely, in both submissive cultures, Mexico and the Orient, existence was perceived as painful and to be endured; man was threatened with pain from birth and was doomed to pain and painful rebirths. Hence, man did not strive for immortality, on the contrary, he sought death to free himself from pain. In Mexico, man was to be systematically defeated, humiliated, captured and offered as live sacrifice to the bloodthirsty unforgiving gods to avert or delay the total and definitive destruction of the universe. Man's beating heart was wrenched from his chest like an apple plucked from a tree, and placed on a Chak god's dish on top of the pyramid. Mexican poetry defined man as "an ephemeral flower, here today and gone tomorrow". The Mexican man had little control over his world or personal life. Predictably, entire civilizations perished overnight without explanation.

In the Orient, the third noble truth of Buddhism suggested that man should exercise total control over his cravings in order to protect himself from spiritual pain and in order to attain the culture valued spiritual triumph: enlightenment. Paradise was defined as the only state through which mortals may escape from painful rebirth: the Nirvana state. In India, self-containment made the apple so forbidden that it was transformed animistically into the sacred cow. The social correlate of the sacredness of the cow was total self restraint, acceptance of established leadership, and of the status quo. In China, this attitude led to the monumental communal effort necessary for the erection of the great wall. In India, it led to the creation and perpetuation of the social inequities of the caste system. Absence of social strife deprived the society of social evolution, but it fostered the exploration of the psychic space and the victory of mind over body.

Each of the four cultures succinctly presented above has generated, through the dynamics of self fulfilling prophecy, its own total environment. All subjects of the system were immersed in its moral imperatives as absolute unquestioned values. In parallel, our contemporary world is dominating its citizens with religious, political, and psychological ideologies. The formal theoretical interpretation of cultural, religious, political, and psychological paradigms addresses the fact that we are all existing in a world of uninterpreted metaphors, a world of popularly endorsed cultural illusions.

| | Disagree | | | | Agree | |
|---|---|---|---|---|---|---|
| 68. I transgress, that is, I do forbidden things or break rules | -3 | -2 | -1 | +1 | +2 | +3 |
| Provocativeness Average Item Score | ______ | | | | | |

**Negative to Counseling and Communication**

| | | | | | | |
|---|---|---|---|---|---|---|
| 69. I do not care what others think of me | -3 | -2 | -1 | +1 | +2 | +3 |
| 70. Nobody understands what therapists are talking about | -3 | -2 | -1 | +1 | +2 | +3 |
| Antitherapy Average Item Score | ______ | | | | | |

## SUBMISSIVE COOPERATIVE SYNDROME

**Cooperation, Trust**

| | | | | | | |
|---|---|---|---|---|---|---|
| 71. People like me for being easy going and low key | -3 | -2 | -1 | +1 | +2 | +3 |
| 72. I never express any anger | -3 | -2 | -1 | +1 | +2 | +3 |
| 73. People think that I am very modest | -3 | -2 | -1 | +1 | +2 | +3 |
| 74. I can take criticism well | -3 | -2 | -1 | +1 | +2 | +3 |
| 75. I have confidence and trust in others | -3 | -2 | -1 | +1 | +2 | +3 |
| 76. I am liked by people in authority | -3 | -2 | -1 | +1 | +2 | +3 |
| Trust Average Item Score | ______ | | | | | |

**Compassion, Considerateness**

| | | | | | | |
|---|---|---|---|---|---|---|
| 77. Even when someone is obnoxious I feel compassion | -3 | -2 | -1 | +1 | +2 | +3 |
| 78. When I say something negative, I always balance it out with something complimentary | -3 | -2 | -1 | +1 | +2 | +3 |
| 79. I remember compliments really well | -3 | -2 | -1 | +1 | +2 | +3 |
| Compassion Average Item Score | ______ | | | | | |

**Respect for Limits**

| | | | | | | |
|---|---|---|---|---|---|---|
| 80. I respect and obey rules and regulations | -3 | -2 | -1 | +1 | +2 | +3 |

**Recessivity**

| | | | | | | |
|---|---|---|---|---|---|---|
| 81. I have difficulty asking people to consider my needs | -3 | -2 | -1 | +1 | +2 | +3 |
| 82. In my relationships I am usually dominated by others | -3 | -2 | -1 | +1 | +2 | +3 |
| 83. I am not rebellious | -3 | -2 | -1 | +1 | +2 | +3 |
| 84. I am the one who gives in and makes concessions first | -3 | -2 | -1 | +1 | +2 | +3 |
| 85. I accommodate others | -3 | -2 | -1 | +1 | +2 | +3 |
| 86. I find it futile arguing | -3 | -2 | -1 | +1 | +2 | +3 |
| 87. I am willing to make changes | -3 | -2 | -1 | +1 | +2 | +3 |
| 88. I do things to please others rather than myself | -3 | -2 | -1 | +1 | +2 | +3 |

# FOUR DISTINCT PERSPECTIVES FOR RAISING THE PENDULUM BALL OF HUMANITY

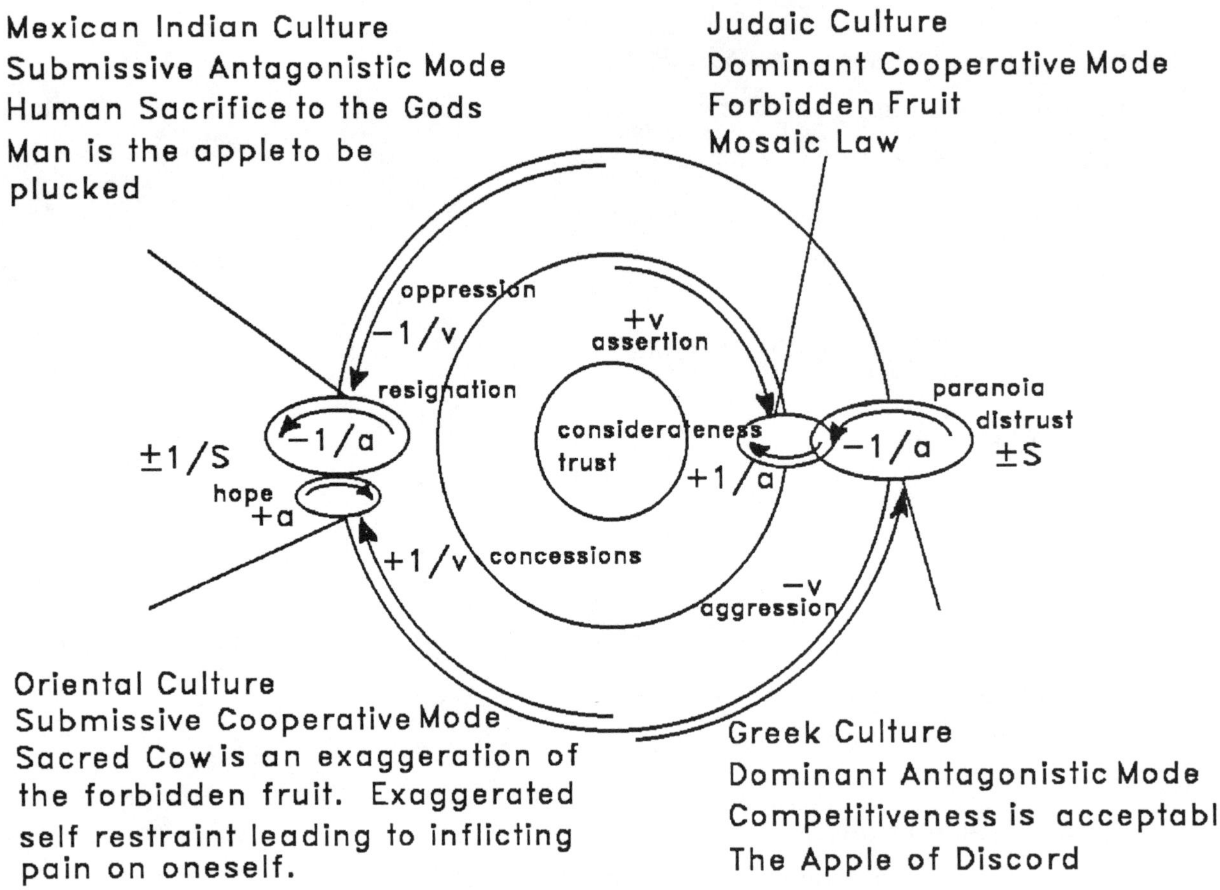


## RELEVANCE OF THE FORMAL THEORY:

The impact of this novel methodological analytical approach will be felt throughout the sciences of man, humanities and social sciences alike. Formal analysis of systems zeroes in on the structural analysis of metaphors as Conflict Resolution Process units. Accordingly, cultural, religious, political, philosophical outlooks, psychological models are analyzed formally as distinct solutions in the realm of formal alternatives. Focusing on interpreting metaphors, the Formal Theory offers a new way of looking at individual behavior for diagnostic and therapeutic purposes. Also it offers a new way of viewing a play or artwork and listening to a composition; what emerges is a new literary analytical approach to works as systems of order. Part of this analytical perspective, the formal approach offers a synthetic perspective to integrate the diversity of alternative compositions or paintings of one artist, the behaviors of one patient, the symbolic universes of one entity, or the totality of cultural and political alternatives, as particular solutions of one basic system of formally related solutions. The Formal Theory integrates various perspectives, reconciles them, but it also offers critical evaluation of the isolated perspective, be that culture, religion, or an author's viewpoint. It examines the isolated perspective's strengths and weaknesses as those of a relationally biased process of conflict resolution.

## THE FORMAL THEORY REDEFINES HEALTH AND JUSTICE AS THE OPTIMAL STRUCTURING OF RELATIONS

The formal theoretical analysis also promotes recognition of the optimal efficient conflict resolution structuring of relations. The Formal Theory, recognizing psychopathology as systemic processes but also health as the engineering of optimal relationships, accordingly places value on economic criteria that confer efficiency and stability to a system. Ethics, health, and politics are redefined as parallel and equivalent searches for order, as the optimal structuring of intra- and interpersonal processes.

| | Disagree | | | | | Agree |
|---|---|---|---|---|---|---|
| 89. I deal with angry people, not by confronting them, but by leaving them alone | -3 | -2 | -1 | +1 | +2 | +3 |
| 90. I'd rather keep peace than express my feelings | -3 | -2 | -1 | +1 | +2 | +3 |
| 91. I don't tell the truth when I think it will make somebody angry | -3 | -2 | -1 | +1 | +2 | +3 |
| 92. I am apologetic | -3 | -2 | -1 | +1 | +2 | +3 |
| 93. I need everyone to like me | -3 | -2 | -1 | +1 | +2 | +3 |
| 94. I am a non-assertive person | -3 | -2 | -1 | +1 | +2 | +3 |
| Recessivity Average Item Score | ______ | | | | | |

**SUBMISSIVE ANTAGONISTIC SYNDROME**

**Communicational Restraint**

| | | | | | | |
|---|---|---|---|---|---|---|
| 95. I find it difficult to say what I feel or what I think for fear of hurting somebody | -3 | -2 | -1 | +1 | +2 | +3 |
| 96. I don't know how to express myself without upsetting people | -3 | -2 | -1 | +1 | +2 | +3 |
| 97. I keep my anger under control. I don't let myself fly off the handle | -3 | -2 | -1 | +1 | +2 | +3 |
| 98. I hold everything in | -3 | -2 | -1 | +1 | +2 | +3 |
| 99. I brood about things that bother me | -3 | -2 | -1 | +1 | +2 | +3 |
| 100. If I have a complaint, it takes me a long time to bring it up | -3 | -2 | -1 | +1 | +2 | +3 |
| 101. Very frequently I am mad and I don't let anyone know it | -3 | -2 | -1 | +1 | +2 | +3 |
| 102. I am an observer at social meetings, not an outspoken participant. | -3 | -2 | -1 | +1 | +2 | +3 |
| 103. I usually don't have much to talk about | -3 | -2 | -1 | +1 | +2 | +3 |
| 104. I am an extremely private person | -3 | -2 | -1 | +1 | +2 | +3 |
| 105. It is difficult for me to relate to others spontaneously | -3 | -2 | -1 | +1 | +2 | +3 |
| 106. People have to pry things out of me | -3 | -2 | -1 | +1 | +2 | +3 |
| 107. I am consistently unable to talk to my partners about what I have on my mind | -3 | -2 | -1 | +1 | +2 | +3 |
| Communicational Restraint Average Item Score | ______ | | | | | |

**Worthlessness, Inferiority**

| | | | | | | |
|---|---|---|---|---|---|---|
| 108. I constantly underestimate my worth and importance | -3 | -2 | -1 | +1 | +2 | +3 |

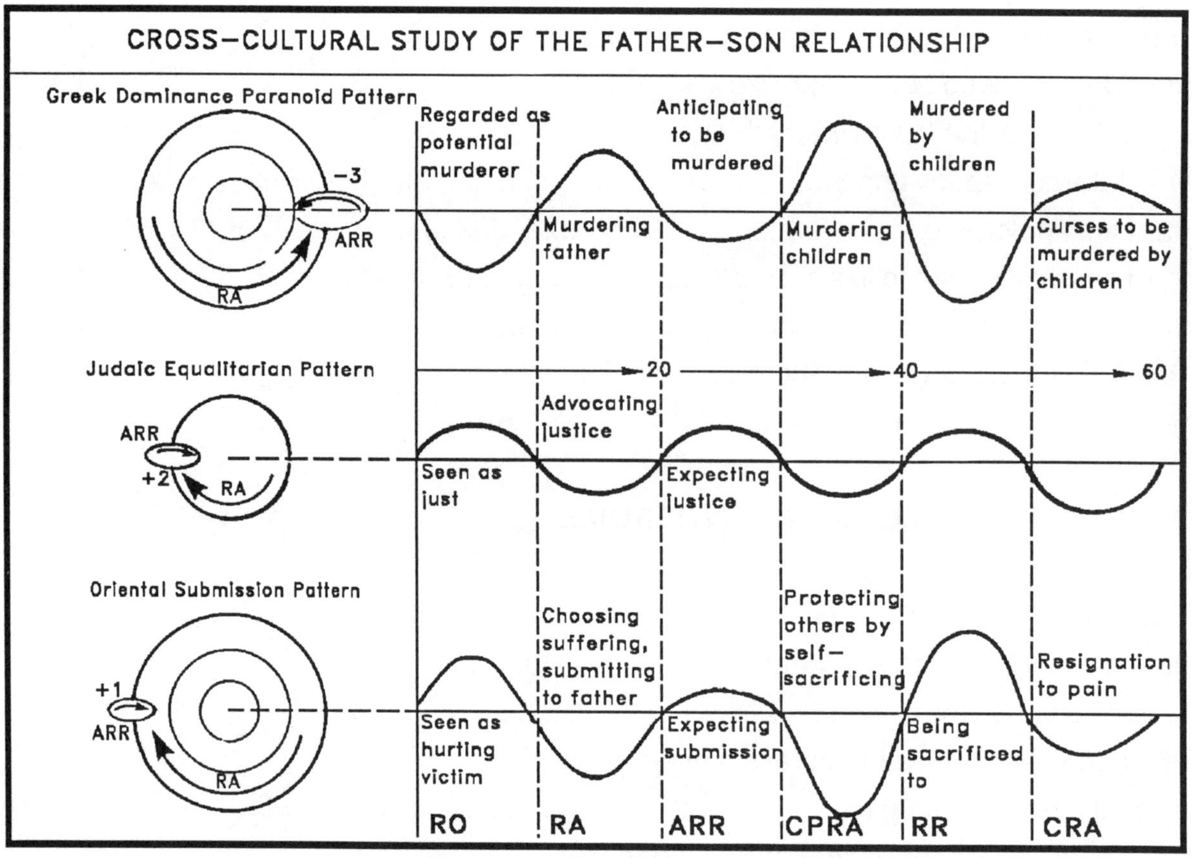


**Diagram 5:** In his actualization and role fulfillments (*RA)* the Greek child is a challenger. He seeks joy and power, sometimes at the expense of his father. The Jewish child seeks justice and partnerships. The Oriental child is totally respectful of his parent and he seeks a guru, a spirital leader. These individuals as parents deal with their children differently (*CPRA)* according to their expectations (*ARR),* and as their children grow they have their expectations fulfilled (*RR).* The Greek son is a challenger to his father; the Judaic son is a partner to his father, while the Oriental child submits to the will of the deified ancestors as well as to that of his own father. Accordingly, the resolution of the father-son relationship (*CRA)* will vary. The Greek parent may curse his offspring, the Judaic will bless them, and the Oriental will seek to experience serenity, entering Nirvana where hopefully the cycle of rebirth through reincarnation will stop and the individual will find eternal freedom from earthly pain.

| | | Disagree | | | | Agree |
|---|---|---|---|---|---|---|
| 109. I have a tendency to put myself down rather than say I do anything that is good, right, or helpful | -3 | -2 | -1 | +1 | +2 | +3 |
| 110. I think people don't like me | -3 | -2 | -1 | +1 | +2 | +3 |
| 111. I frequently mumble or whisper when I speak | -3 | -2 | -1 | +1 | +2 | +3 |
| 112. If somebody doesn't hear what I say, I say, "Forget it." | -3 | -2 | -1 | +1 | +2 | +3 |
| 113. I can't stick up for myself | -3 | -2 | -1 | +1 | +2 | +3 |
| 114. In most of my relationships I am the person who gets pushed around | -3 | -2 | -1 | +1 | +2 | +3 |
| 115. I am afraid I might bore people with my conversation | -3 | -2 | -1 | +1 | +2 | +3 |
| 116. People don't care about what I think and how I feel | -3 | -2 | -1 | +1 | +2 | +3 |
| 117. I am always expecting criticism and disapproval | -3 | -2 | -1 | +1 | +2 | +3 |
| 118. People laugh at me behind my back | -3 | -2 | -1 | +1 | +2 | +3 |
| Inferiority Average Item Score | ______ | | | | | |
| **Resignation without Hostility** | | | | | | |
| 119. I have difficulty facing conflict. I run away from things | -3 | -2 | -1 | +1 | +2 | +3 |
| 120. I've given up trying to control things in my life | -3 | -2 | -1 | +1 | +2 | +3 |
| 121. I want to be left alone | -3 | -2 | -1 | +1 | +2 | +3 |
| 122. The image I present to people is one of "I don't want to be here." | -3 | -2 | -1 | +1 | +2 | +3 |
| 123. I never win an argument | -3 | -2 | -1 | +1 | +2 | +3 |
| 124. I never get angry, I just get bored | -3 | -2 | -1 | +1 | +2 | +3 |
| 125. I tend to tune out when people attack me | -3 | -2 | -1 | +1 | +2 | +3 |
| 126. I have difficulty establishing satisfactory long-term relationships. | -3 | -2 | -1 | +1 | +2 | +3 |
| 127. Considering therapy depresses me | -3 | -2 | -1 | +1 | +2 | +3 |
| Resignation #1 Average Item Score | ______ | | | | | |
| **Resignation with Hostility** | | | | | | |
| 128. I give in to my partners but I resent them | -3 | -2 | -1 | +1 | +2 | +3 |
| 129. I let others make me do things I don't agree with | -3 | -2 | -1 | +1 | +2 | +3 |
| 130. Others frequently initiate and control my activities. | -3 | -2 | -1 | +1 | +2 | +3 |
| 131. In my relationships I am the passive and hostile partner | -3 | -2 | -1 | +1 | +2 | +3 |
| Resignation #2 Average Item Score | ______ | | | | | |
| **Hostility** | | | | | | |
| 132. I frequently say negative things | -3 | -2 | -1 | +1 | +2 | +3 |
| 133. I laugh at others behind their backs | -3 | -2 | -1 | +1 | +2 | +3 |

In the submissive antagonistic manner Mexican man is inflicting pain on his fellow man.

Sacrificing to the Sun God, a priest plunges a knife into the chest of a warrior, whose soul is seen ascending skyward in a bloody trail.

By contrast, in the submissive cooperative manner the Oriental man strives for cessation of desires by inflicting pain on himself. The starving Indian man disregards the "apple" as an opportunity to satisfy his needs by animistically transforming it into the sacred identities and institutions which he revers as more venerable than his own needs desires and cravings.

**POWERLESSNESS AND PAIN - LOSS OF LIFE - ATTAINED COOPERATIVELY (INDIA) AND ANTAGONISTICALLY (MEXICO)**

The Sacred Cow of India, Drawn by A. de Neuville

Indian Devotees- Jogees wounding themselves, Drawn by Emile Bayard

| | Disagree | | | | Agree | |
|---|---|---|---|---|---|---|
| 134. All I convey is cracks, zingers and zappers | -3 | -2 | -1 | +1 | +2 | +3 |
| 135. I frequently feel hostile but say nothing | -3 | -2 | -1 | +1 | +2 | +3 |
| 136. I resent authorities and I quietly undermine them | -3 | -2 | -1 | +1 | +2 | +3 |
| 137. I resent others telling me what to do | -3 | -2 | -1 | +1 | +2 | +3 |
| 138. I don't listen | -3 | -2 | -1 | +1 | +2 | +3 |
| 139. I am vindictive | -3 | -2 | -1 | +1 | +2 | +3 |
| 140. I am secretive and suspicious | -3 | -2 | -1 | +1 | +2 | +3 |
| Hostility Average Item Score | ________ | | | | | |

**PSYCHIC TENSION -**

**INTENSITY OF CONFLICT EXPERIENCED**

**Anxiety Level**

| | | | | | | |
|---|---|---|---|---|---|---|
| 141. I am anxious most of the time | -3 | -2 | -1 | +1 | +2 | +3 |
| 142. I suffer from severe anxiety under special circumstances | -3 | -2 | -1 | +1 | +2 | +3 |
| 143. I am too sensitive, nothing passes over my head | -3 | -2 | -1 | +1 | +2 | +3 |
| Anxiety Average Item Score | ________ | | | | | |

**Family History**

| | | | | | | |
|---|---|---|---|---|---|---|
| 144. A number of my blood relatives have suffered from severe emotional problems | -3 | -2 | -1 | +1 | +2 | +3 |

**Duration of Disability**

| | | | | | | |
|---|---|---|---|---|---|---|
| 145. I have been unable to cope for a long time | - 3 | -2 | -1 | +1 | +2 | +3 |
| 146. It is only recently that I have been unable to function | -3 | -2 | -1 | +1 | +2 | +3 |
| Disability Duration Average Item Score | ________ | | | | | |

**Intensity of Disability**

| | | | | | | |
|---|---|---|---|---|---|---|
| 147. I am having difficulty functioning around the house | -3 | -2 | -1 | +1 | +2 | +3 |
| 148. I have retreated to my own private world | -3 | -2 | -1 | +1 | +2 | +3 |
| 149. I tend to tune out rather than deal with an unpleasant reality. | -3 | -2 | -1 | +1 | +2 | +3 |
| 150. I am afraid of having a mental breakdown | -3 | -2 | -1 | +1 | +2 | +3 |
| 151. My feelings scare me | -3 | -2 | -1 | +1 | +2 | +3 |
| 152. I am afraid of losing control of myself | -3 | -2 | -1 | +1 | +2 | +3 |
| 153. I am preoccupied with thoughts of hurting somebody | -3 | -2 | -1 | +1 | +2 | +3 |
| 154. I've given up trying to control things in my life | -3 | -2 | -1 | +1 | +2 | +3 |
| 155. I dwell on certain thoughts for long hours | -3 | -2 | -1 | +1 | +2 | +3 |
| Disability Intensity Average Item Score | ________ | | | | | |

In the dominant cooperative mode the Judaic man is aspiring for the apple, but is concerned about divine punishment as illustrated in the biblical creation story. A painting of Adam and Eve by Cornelis Cornelisz Van Haarlem

**POWER OR PLEASURE - ATTAINED COOPERATIVELY (JUDEA) OR ANTAGONISTICALLY (GREECE)**

In the dominant antagonistic mode, Greek man pursues the apple as a trophy, as the confirmation of his capacity to dominate his counterparts.

"Hera, Aphrodite, and Athena rushed to pick the apple up, each one thinking herself the fairest. It was not a golden apple of love that Eris had thrown, but the apple of discord, and the three goddesses began to quarrel about who should have it.", from Greek Myths, Doubleday and Company Inc.
Art by Ingri and Edgar Parin D'aulaire

| **Phobic Thinking** | Disagree | | | | | Agree |
|---|---|---|---|---|---|---|
| 156. I can no longer control my fears. They control me........ | -3 | -2 | -1 | +1 | +2 | +3 |
| 157. I am handicapped by my phobias, fears, andcompulsions........................................................... | -3 | -2 | -1 | +1 | +2 | +3 |
| Phobic Average Item Score | ______ | | | | | |
| **Depression** | | | | | | |
| 158. I do a lot of crying....................................................... | -3 | -2 | -1 | +1 | +2 | +3 |
| 159. I repeatedly wake up at night and have difficulty fallingasleep................................................................ | -3 | -2 | -1 | +1 | +2 | +3 |
| 160. I suffer from nightmares............................................. | -3 | -2 | -1 | +1 | +2 | +3 |
| 161. I am overwhelmed with guilt for certain things I have done................................................................ | -3 | -2 | -1 | +1 | +2 | +3 |
| 162. I get upset with very little provocation........................... | -3 | -2 | -1 | +1 | +2 | +3 |
| 163. I am ready to give up................................................... | -3 | -2 | -1 | +1 | +2 | +3 |
| 164. I am preoccupied with thoughts of hurting myself......... | -3 | -2 | -1 | +1 | +2 | +3 |
| Depression Average Item Score | ______ | | | | | |
| **Degree of Self-Consciousness** | | | | | | |
| 165. I experience at times incomprehensible psychic phenomena.......................................................... | -3 | -2 | -1 | +1 | +2 | +3 |
| 166. I have experienced illusions of greatness..................... | -3 | -2 | -1 | +1 | +2 | +3 |
| 167. I have heard voices telling me what to do...................... | -3 | -2 | -1 | +1 | +2 | +3 |
| 168. I have heard voices calling my name............................ | -3 | -2 | -1 | +1 | +2 | +3 |
| 169. I feel as if I'm under surveillance.................................. | -3 | -2 | -1 | +1 | +2 | +3 |
| 170. I feel that people are staring at me.............................. | -3 | -2 | -1 | +1 | +2 | +3 |
| 171. I am very self-conscious............................................. | -3 | -2 | -1 | +1 | +2 | +3 |
| 172. Occasionally I feel that my house is transparent........... | -3 | -2 | -1 | +1 | +2 | +3 |
| 173. I feel that my life is controlled by external forces............ | -3 | -2 | -1 | +1 | +2 | +3 |
| 174. I believe colors or numbers have magic meanings....... | -3 | -2 | -1 | +1 | +2 | +3 |
| 175. I feel as if people are trying to get me............................ | -3 | -2 | -1 | +1 | +2 | +3 |
| Self-Consciousness Average Item Score | ______ | | | | | |
| **Particular Areas of Conflict** | | | | | | |
| 176. I have a split personality............................................. | -3 | -2 | -1 | +1 | +2 | +3 |
| 177. I suffer from an uncontrollable compulsion to eat excessively. ................................................................ | -3 | -2 | -1 | +1 | +2 | +3 |
| 178. I am anorexic. I control my eating to the point that I have lost too much weight........................................... | -3 | -2 | -1 | +1 | +2 | +3 |
| 179. I have a serious weight problem.................................. | -3 | -2 | -1 | +1 | +2 | +3 |
| 180. I suffer from an unmanageable drug habit..................... | -3 | -2 | -1 | +1 | +2 | +3 |

## MICRO AND MACRO VALIDATIONS OF THE FORMAL THEORY THROUGH THE FORMAL INTERPRETATION OF METAPHORS

### THE GORSKI CANVASES MAY BE INTEGRATED INTO THE CONTINUUM OF A PERSONAL CONFLICT RESOLUTION PROCESS

On the jacket of the first volume, Level 1 of the Gorski Retrospective, we have a demonstration of the formal integration of symbolic transformations in an artist's universe. The four canvases featured on the cover represent four relationally distinct perspectives in the interpretation of the same reality, the theme of the mouth, as they evolved sequentially and spontaneously in the course of twelve years. This formal integration of diversity exemplifies dramatically a prototype manifestation of the Conflict Resolution Process. In the chronological evolution of these canvases we witness the gradual reduction of conflict and the attainment of internal order, that is, of identity or spirituality.

The angry, paranoid presentation of "Consumer, Consumed, Consumed", dated 1962, represents the inception of a conflict, visualized as the experience of an intensely uncomfortable emotional state. The determined "Eye-dentity" canvas, dated 1974, coincides with the attainment of the conflict's resolution. It presents the acceptance of pain combined with a sense of integrity, personal stability, and luminous harmony. The inception and resolution of conflict canvases as end states dramatizes two diverse structurings of authority relations. The conflicted aggressive, dominant antagonistic expression is contrasting strongly with the peaceful, loving, dominant cooperative alternative. Instead of man consuming and being consumed, he chooses to be a creator who accepts the pain of the crucifixion and who is accepting the halos of holiness and enlightenment.

According to the Formal Theory, these two end states are not haphazardly determined, aesthetically pleasing, and purely informational statements. Formally, they are dialectically related energetic states determined by the necessity of the underlying Conflict Resolution Process. The canvases portray qualitatively distinct energetic modality states; the initial one of intense social-personal conflict corresponds to labile psychic energy, while the latter, indicating psychosocial integration, corresponds to conflict resolution, a stabler energetic state. Identity formation coincides with the reduction of personal conflict, the harmonization of the individual with the social system, the surrendering of individual deviance or antagonism and paranoia for a harmonious merging with the social system. The repetition of the Conflict Resolution Process in three separate thematically homogenous Gorski symbolic universes confirms the existence of the Conflict Resolution Process in mental phenomena.

The Formal Theory reduces the aesthetic and psychologically meaningful phenomena of conflict resolution into formal and natural scientific terms. The art forms evolve with scientific predictability and natural science determinism. Relational perspectives have physical energetic underpinnings which determine this evolutional process and define its aesthetic parameters. Thus, underlying the art and psychology of the Conflict Resolution Process is natural or physical necessity, a paramount need to reduce disorder or labile energy to attain stability through harmonization of the individual and the system. The Gorski exhibit demonstrates that creativity conserves energy through symbolic energetic transformations and that it leads to the upgrading of energy from conflict or entropy to the higher form of meaning or endelecy. (See Volume VIII)

### CULTURAL PARADIGMS MAY BE FORMALLY INTEGRATED INTO A UNIVERSE OF FORMALLY EVOLVING FAMILY POLITICS

Equivalent to the integration of diversity in the disparate Gorski paintings through the Conflict Resolution Process, we may detect formal evolutionary continuity and determinism among the disparate topical cultural authority resolutions as these are portrayed in the Preface of the volume under the exercise of integration of cultural metaphors. The four cultures may be conceived as representing a dynamically integrated continuum of evolving personal Conflict Resolution Processes or identity formations. There is evidence confirming this hypothesis in the fact that we may detect formal continuity among the four cultures in spite of the fact that they appear to be merely separate parallel anthropological developments. We also have evidence that one culture evolved independently through some of these phases, e.g., the Greek culture has had a matriarchal, a patriarchal, a moon goddess, and a sun god phases. The continuity among the four paradigms may be detected by considering the topical cultural solutions as formally related alternatives of the basic family interpersonal dynamics. Accordingly, we may hypothesize that the evolutionary sequence began as shifts of central power from the Earth Mother goddess to the Heavenly Father god to the daughter/mother/Moon goddess identity, eventually to the son as the Sun god by himself. Finally the power was distributed equitably among the entire family, including the mother, father, and the children.

First, in order of precedence in the context of the four cultures depicted, we recognize the American Indian, in particular pre-Columbian Mexican culture with its life sacrificial rituals. In this paradigm power rests with the primordial mother goddess, Coatlique (Mother Earth) who is paranoid of her moralistic daughter, Quoyatsacli (the Moon) and her other children (the Stars). She is protected from them by her parthenogenetically emerging warrior son, Huitzilopochtli (the Sun God) who, upon his arrival, murders his siblings, the Moon and the Stars, which are still daily eclipsed upon sunrise. This power structure permeated all aspects of the Mexican cultural system. (See Volume II of Normative Publications)

Possibly the second step in this evolutionary sequence is the ancient Greek culture which represents the shifting of power from the paranoid mother to the evolving son, Huitzilopochtli, who in Greece becomes a dominant, antagonistic, and paranoid father. In the Greek cosmogony, to defend them from their father, mother Earth allied herself protectively with her children. While Olympus was equally divided between six male and six female divinities, the family dynamics remained unsettled. The marital dyad was torn by strife and

| | Disagree | | | | | Agree |
|---|---|---|---|---|---|---|
| 181. I suffer from a sexual dysfunction | -3 | -2 | -1 | +1 | +2 | +3 |
| 182. Some people think I abuse alcohol | -3 | -2 | -1 | +1 | +2 | +3 |
| 183. I am physically attracted to people of the same sex | -3 | -2 | -1 | +1 | +2 | +3 |
| 184. I have a strong need to repeatedly wash my hands, check on appliances and on having locked all doors | -3 | -2 | -1 | +1 | +2 | +3 |
| 185. Frequently I worry about my health and fear I am going to die | -3 | -2 | -1 | +1 | +2 | +3 |
| 186. I get in trouble with people in authority | -3 | -2 | -1 | +1 | +2 | +3 |
| 187. I have gotten in trouble with the law | -3 | -2 | -1 | +1 | +2 | +3 |

Areas of Conflict Average Item Score ____________________

**Psychosomatic Conditions**

| | | | | | | |
|---|---|---|---|---|---|---|
| 188. I have suffered from one or more of the following conditions (underline): high blood pressure, asthma, migraine headaches, ulcers, colitis, diarrhea, allergies, other | -3 | -2 | -1 | +1 | +2 | +3 |
| 189. I suffer from an epileptic condition | -3 | -2 | -1 | +1 | +2 | +3 |
| 190. I have suffered from cycles of deep depression followed by extraordinary highs, each phase of this cycle lasting for periods of weeks or months at a time. When depressed I have felt on the brink of suicide; when high I have been unreasonable, wreckless and so full of energy that I can't sleep | -3 | -2 | -1 | +1 | +2 | +3 |

(Underline what is pertinent)

Psychosomatic Average Item Score ____________________

**Degree of Relational Stability**

| | | | | | | |
|---|---|---|---|---|---|---|
| 191. I am so insecure that I constantly seek reassurance, approval, and praise | -3 | -2 | -1 | +1 | +2 | +3 |
| 192. I am perfectionistic. My expectations of myself are so high that they interfere with my completing ordinary assignments | -3 | -2 | -1 | +1 | +2 | +3 |
| 193. I am emotionally unstable. In a short period of time and without much provocation, my moods change back and forth from silly laughter to irritability, anger and tears | -3 | -2 | -1 | +1 | +2 | +3 |
| 194. Instead of taking the time to develop meaningful and lasting relationships, I get involved in fleeting and superficial relationships | -3 | -2 | -1 | +1 | +2 | +3 |

Relational Stability Average Item Score ____________________ extramarital intrigue. Athena at the end of the consmogony cycles represents the new compromise in the battle of the sexes for control of the family. The power struggle between the Mexican paranoid mother and the Greek paranoid fathers yielded a virginal goddess of the patron of the emerging Athenian civilization. Ongoing power struggles and intense conflict process were prevalent in the matrimonial dyad of the Greek mortals. Paranoid Greek men, brothers Agamemnon, Menelaus and the Greek coalition of kings, pursued the defiant Moon goddess equivalents, sisters Helen, Klytemnestra, and daughter Iphigenia along the pathway carved by the moon goddess, Ios (Helen and Ios mean moon). Helen followed Ios' trail to Troy. Ios was a woman made pregnant by Zeus, transformed into a cow by Hera, chased by Hera's emissary, Argos Panoptes turned into a gadfly (later into a peacock); the cow fled from the Greek mainland over Bosporus (the Jump of the Cow) to Asia Minor, or Troy. Troy represented the bastion of the emerging embattled motherhood. Elsewhere, I have theorized that mother Helen escaped Mt. Taygetus, from which children were killed, to pursue asylum in a land, Troy, which was friendly to motherhood.(Page 36 - Volume I)

Territorially, the Asian continent has been dominated by cultural models in which the daughter/mother/moon goddess, the reign of the daughter who became mother, have emerged to the status of sacredness. This represents the third phase of family political evolution. The cult of the powerful moon goddess/sacred cow and the protected monkey coincided with the emasculation and total spiritualization of the male sexual passion. The Orient has promoted total male self-containment, that is, the suppression of cravings or desires as the condition of nirvana, the state of non-rebirth.

By contrast, in Egypt power gravitated to the sacredness of the son/Sun god/father figure. Pharaohs were deified, and as gods, they enjoyed during afterlife the companionship of sacrificed women and slaves buried with the dead king. The foundation of introspective divine monotheism in Egypt was a step toward moderation of male power in the family system. The asian extreme feminism and suppressed male chauvinism of the Orient were balanced by prevalence of the introspective male dominance in Egypt.

In Mesopotamia, the extremes of the male sun and the female moon dominated religions merged dialectically to lead to partner parity. In this environment family role fairness and acceptable, liberated, but family contained sexuality prevailed. The nomadic Semites accomplished this blending in Judaism where the sacredness was shifted in the man-god parity formally established in the concept of the ***covenant***. The ***covenant*** between Abraham and God reflected another twist in the evolving democratization of family politics. The ***covenant*** is evidence of a spirit of cooperation and ongoing negotiations among all members of the family unit projected into the divine reference. The Bible is an epic of family relations evolving toward developing the optimal structuring of family role relations. This evolution obeyed the constitution spelled out by the Mosaic Law, the morality of the Ten Commandments, the legislation of cooperative behavior toward attainment of peace, shalom, the maximal reduction of conflict. It seems as though conflict resolution, as the most efficient and stable sociological and psychological distribution of power was the evolutionary objective of the ongoing anthropological exploration.

In a number of incidents of the families of the Patriarchs, especially of Abraham, Sarah, and Isaac we witness the consolidation of the ***covenant as a social contract of family relations***. A key demonstration of this spirit was the handling of male extramarital relations as reflected in Sarah's request that Abraham part ways with her rival, Hagar, and her son, Ishmael, and ***Abraham's willingness*** to respect and consent to this request. Reciprocally Sarah consented to weaning herself from their son Isaac and letting Abraham, the father, have the prerogative of testing his son's loyalty by suggesting his immolation. Abraham's willingness to obey God and Isaac's willingness to ascend the pyre, the Akeda, proved that fathers and sons were partners rather than rivals. The ***covenant*** was a family social contract which entailed that mother, father, and children were equally respected members of a cooperative system. The Judaic tradition evolved rituals for self-monitoring and self-restraint blended with clearly expressed gratitude. Moral accountability and responsibility for the welfare of others became social virtues in this cultural environment. Marital sexuality coincided with love in the power balanced, relatively peaceful Judaic marital system.

In our contemporary times, because of the lack of scientific humanities, we are experiencing a moral and ethical pluralism bordering on agnosticism. In this moral vacuum, religious, political, and psychological models have become the moral forces arbitrarily determining normative, that is, ethical behavior. (For more information, see Volume I, pagees xxvi,352)

**CONFLICT ANALYSIS BATTERY**



**TRANSPARENT MASK TEST (TMT)**

Name:________________________

Date:______________Age:_______

Step 1: In the space below draw a mask.

**Step 2**: Answer the following questions:

Give the mask a title__________________________________________

Age:_____Sex:______What emotions does this mask convey?

_______________________________________________________________

_______________________________________________________________

**Step 3:** What are the conflicts represented in this mask?

_______________________________________________________________

_______________________________________________________________

**Step 4**: What resolution of conflicts does this mask represent?

_______________________________________________________________

_______________________________________________________________

**Step 5:** Imagine that the mask you drew has become transparent. Make a drawing of what you see through the mask, reflecting true feelings.

Fill in the blanks and answer the questions:

**Step 6**: Name or title ______________________________________________

Age:____ Sex:____ What emotions does this mask convey?

______________________________________________________________________

______________________________________________________________________

**Step 7:** What conflicts does this drawing represent?

______________________________________________________________________

______________________________________________________________________

**Step 8:** What resolution of conflicts does it convey?

______________________________________________________________________

______________________________________________________________________

**Step 9:** Make a drawing of what you see in this person's heart. Indicate this figuratively, portraying conflicts or using colors reflecting this person's emotions.

Answer the following questions:

**Title:**________________________________________

**Step 10:** Indicate items and themes represented in the drawing.

________________________________________________

________________________________________________

**Step 11**: Elaborate on what feelings and conflicts this drawing represents.

________________________________________________

________________________________________________

**Step 12**: What resolution of conflicts does it convey?

________________________________________________

________________________________________________

You have completed the Transparent Mask imagery test.

**Step 13**: Give a title to the sequence:

______________________________________________________________

**Step 14**: Summarize here the sequence of transformations of these images.

______________________________________________________________
______________________________________________________________
______________________________________________________________
______________________________________________________________

**Step 15**: What are your conclusions about the way this person resolves conflicts?

______________________________________________________________
______________________________________________________________
______________________________________________________________

**Step 16**: How does that progression relate to your feelings and choices you have in handling feelings?

______________________________________________________________
______________________________________________________________
______________________________________________________________

**Step 17:** What changes should you make in the way you communicate your feelings?

______________________________________________________________
______________________________________________________________
______________________________________________________________

**Step 18**: What changes are you willing to make in order to reduce the intensity of these conflicts?

______________________________________________________________
______________________________________________________________
______________________________________________________________
______________________________________________________________

**CONFLICT ANALYSIS BATTERY**



Name:________________________

Date:______________ Age:________

**BALLOON PORTRAITS AND STORY**

**(BP+S)**

**(FAMILY OF ORIGIN, MARITAL FAMILY)**

**Step 1**: Please make a portrait of your family of origin by drawing and coloring balloons to depict each member of the group. Include yourself in this family portrait. Feel free to be imaginative with the configurations, the shapes, the colors, the placement of the balloons. Allow your feelings about the members of the family to show through these drawings. Indicate under each balloon the relationship (father, sister, etc.) and each person's approximate age.

**Step 2**: Identify each individual, his/her relationship, his/her age, and personality, listing three characteristics.

Balloon #1: ____________________

#2: ____________________

#3: ____________________

#4: ____________________

#5: ____________________

#6: ____________________

#7: ____________________

#8: ____________________

#9: ____________________

**Step 3**: The balloons are having a conversation. What are they saying to each other?

____________________

____________________

____________________

____________________

____________________

**Step 4**: What were the balloons saying or doing before the conversation you just recorded?

____________________

____________________

**Step 5**: What were the balloons saying or doing after the initial conversation?

____________________

____________________

**Step 6:** Give a title to the story.____________________

**Step 7:** What conflicts are these balloons experiencing?

____________________

____________________

____________________

____________________

____________________

**Step 8**: What changes should be made to resolve these conflicts?

____________________

____________________

____________________

____________________

____________________

____________________

**MARITAL FAMILY BALLOON PORTRAIT**

**Step 1**: Now draw a balloon portrait of your Marital Family. Indicate the relationship to you and the age of each individual.

**Step 2**: Identify three characteristics of each member of the family

Balloon #1:____________________

#2: ____________________

#3: ____________________

#4: ____________________

#5:_ ____________________

**Step 3**: The individuals are conversing. Record their exchanges.

____________________

____________________

____________________

____________________

____________________

____________________

____________________

____________________

**Step 4**: Title:____________________

**Step 5**: What conflicts are these individuals experiencing?

____________________

____________________

____________________

**CONFLICT ANALYSIS BATTERY**



Name:__________________

Date:____________Age:_____

**CONFLICTUAL MEMORIES TEST (CMT)**

**CHILDHOOD, ADOLESCENCE, and PEER CONFLICTS**

**Conflict of Childhood:**

**Step 1:** Please draw and color in a most conflictual memory from your childhood. Feel free to be as imaginative as you wish with the portrayal of this conflict to allow your feelings to show through the drawings.

**Step 2**: Describe the incident. Who was there and what happened?

______________________________________________________________________

______________________________________________________________________

______________________________________________________________________

______________________________________________________________________

______________________________________________________________________

______________________________________________________________________

______________________________________________________________________

______________________________________________________________________

**Step 3:** How did you feel about this person?

How did the person feel about you?

**Step 4**: What were the conflicts involved?

**Step 5**: What happened before?

**Step 6**: What happened after?

**Step 7**: What was your share in creating this conflict?

**Step 8**: How has this experience affected your life?

**Step 9**: Have you been repeating yourself?____________________
**Step 10**: Has this conflict been resolved in your mind?____________________
**Step 11**: Has this conflict been resolved in this relationship?____________________
**Step 12**: What changes could be made to resolve your conflicts, to free yourself from reexperiencing them?

**Step 1: Conflict of Adolescence**: Draw the most conflictual memory of your adolescence.

**Step 2:** Describe the incident.
(Who was there, what happened? What was your share in creating the conflict?)

______________________________________________________________________

______________________________________________________________________

**Step 3:** How has this affected you?

______________________________________________________________________

______________________________________________________________________

**Step 1: Recent Conflict**: Draw the most conflictual recent memory.

**Step 2:** Describe the incident.
(Who was there, what happened? What was your share in creating the conflict?)

______________________________________________________________________

______________________________________________________________________

**Step 3:** How has this affected you?

______________________________________________________________________

______________________________________________________________________

**CONFLICT ANALYSIS BATTERY**



**ANIMAL METAPHOR TEST #1 (AMT#1)**

Name:__________________________

Date:__________________Age:______

This test offers you the opportunity to be imaginative and create a story featuring two animals. To do this, follow these steps:

**Step 1**: Draw two animal figures in color. *Please use pencil or pen to outline and color in using crayons, pencils, or magic markers.*

**Step 2**: Fill in the blanks. *Please use a pen.*

ANIMAL #1

Type of animal:________________

Age in human years:____________

Animal's sex:__________________

Describe the animal's personality by listing 3 or more traits:

__________________________________

__________________________________

__________________________________

ANIMAL #2

Type of animal:_____________________

Age in human years:_________________

Animal's sex:_______________________

Describe the animal's personality by listing 3 or more traits:

______________________________________

______________________________________

______________________________________

**Step 3**: The animals are having a conversation. What are they saying to each other? Indicate the sequence referring to the animals by their identity number.

**Step 4**: What were the animals doing and saying before the conversation just recorded?

**Step 5**: What did your animals do and say after the initial conversation?

______________________________________________________________________

______________________________________________________________________

______________________________________________________________________

______________________________________________________________________

______________________________________________________________________

______________________________________________________________________

**Step 6:** Give a title to the story____________________________________________

**Step 7a**: What conflicts are these animals experiencing between themselves?

______________________________________________________________________

______________________________________________________________________

______________________________________________________________________

______________________________________________________________________

______________________________________________________________________

**Step 7b**: What are the conflicts between them and their world? Elaborate.

______________________________________________________________________

______________________________________________________________________

______________________________________________________________________

______________________________________________________________________

______________________________________________________________________

______________________________________________________________________

**Step 8:** What changes should these animals make to resolve their conflicts?

______________________________________________________________________

______________________________________________________________________

______________________________________________________________________

______________________________________________________________________

______________________________________________________________________

______________________________________________________________________

______________________________________________________________________

______________________________________________________________________

______________________________________________________________________

______________________________________________________________________

______________________________________________________________________

______________________________________________________________________

**Step 9:** Which animal do you identify with most? Elaborate.

Whom do you identify with the counterpart animal? Elaborate.

**Step 10:** How does this animal drama pertain to you?

**Step 11:** What changes should you make to resolve your conflicts?

**Step 12**: In life we repeat ourselves. Present an incident similar to what transpired in your metaphor story to illustrate your particular pattern.

**Step 13:** Reviewing this incident, describe your relational pattern, that is, how you relate with other people, and how you set things up to get yourself in trouble.

**Step 14**: What changes are you willing to make?

**CONFLICT ANALYSIS BATTERY**



**FAIRY TALE METAPHOR TEST (FMT)**

Name:____________________

Date:______________Age:_____

This test offers you the opportunity to be imaginative and create a story featuring two characters from your favorite fairy tale. To do this, follow these steps:

**Step 1**: Draw your two characters in color. *Please use pencil or pen to outline and color in using crayons, pencils, or magic markers.*

**Step 2:** Fill in the blanks. *Please use a pen.*

CHARACTER #1

Character's name:______________

________________________________

Character's age in human years:__________

Character's sex:______________

Character's personality, list3 or more traits:

________________________________________

________________________________________

________________________________________

CHARACTER #2

Character's name:______________________

______________________________________

Character's age in human years:____________

Character's sex:______________

Character's personality, list 3 or more traits:

________________________________________

________________________________________

________________________________________

**Step 3**: The characters are having a conversation. What are they saying to each other? Indicate the sequence with the numbers of the characters, #1 and #2.

**Step 4**: What were the characters doing and saying before the conversation just recorded?

**Step 5**: What did your characters do and say after the initial conversation?

**Step 6**: Give a title to the story________________________________________

**Step 7a:** What conflicts are these characters experiencing between themselves?

**Step 7b:** What are the conflicts between them and their world? Elaborate.

**Step 8**: What changes should these characters make to resolve their conflicts?

**Step 9:** Which character do you identify with most? Elaborate.

Whom do you identify with the counterpart character? Elaborate.

**Step 10**: How does this fairy tale pertain to you?

**Step 11:** What changes should you make to resolve your conflicts?

**Step 12**: In life we repeat ourselves. Present an incident, similar to what transpired in your metaphor story, to illustrate your particular pattern.

**Step 13**: Reviewing this incident, describe your relational pattern, that is, how you relate with other people, and how you set things up to get yourself in trouble.

**Step 14:** What changes are you willing to make?

**CONFLICT ANALYSIS BATTERY**



**SHORT STORY METAPHOR (SSM)**

Name:____________________

Date:_____________Age:_____

**Step 1**: Choose two imaginary characters and write a short story about one of their adventures.

**Step 2:** Make a drawing of the key transaction between the characters and give it a caption. List the characteristics of the story's heroes as you did for the animals in the Animal Metaphor Test.

Character's identity #1:
Character's Name:_______________
Age:______ Sex:______
Three traits describing the personality:
______________________________
______________________________
______________________________
______________________________

Character's identity #2:
Character's Name:_______________
Age:______ Sex:______
Three traits describing the personality:
______________________________
______________________________
______________________________
______________________________

**Step 3**: What had gone on before the adventure?

______________________________________________

______________________________________________

______________________________________________

______________________________________________

______________________________________________

______________________________________________

**Step 4**: What happened after the adventure?

______________________________________________

______________________________________________

______________________________________________

______________________________________________

______________________________________________

**Step 5**: Give a title to the story.______________________________

**Step 6**: What conflicts are these characters experiencing?

______________________________________________

______________________________________________

______________________________________________

______________________________________________

______________________________________________

______________________________________________

**Step 7**: What changes should these characters make to resolve their conflicts?

______________________________________________

______________________________________________

______________________________________________

______________________________________________

______________________________________________

______________________________________________

______________________________________________

______________________________________________

______________________________________________

______________________________________________

______________________________________________

**Step 8**: Which character do you identify with most?

Whom does the other character remind you of?

**Step 9**: How does this short story pertain to you?

**Step 10**: What changes should you make to resolve your conflicts?

**Step 11**: In life we repeat ourselves. Present an incident similar to what transpired in your metaphor to illustrate your particular pattern.

**Step 12:** Reviewing this incident, describe your relational pattern, that is,how you relate with other people, and how you set things up to get yourself in trouble.

**Step 13:** What changes are you willing to make?

**CONFLICT ANALYSIS BATTERY**



**ANIMAL METAPHOR TEST #2 (AMT#2)**

**INTENSIFICATION OF CONFLICT TEST**

Name:________________________

Date:______________Age:______

Recreate your Animal Metaphor Test choosing animals and dialogue that will convey intensification of conflicts between them. Choose an animal that will represent the active state of mind (more aggressive, more vain, more arrogant) and a counterpart animal that will represent the passive state of mind (more scared, more depressed, more in a state of panic, failure or humiliation).**Step 1:** Draw two animal figures in color. *Please use pencil or pen to outline and color in using crayons, pencils ,or magic markers.*

**Step 2:** Fill in the blanks. *Please use a pen.*

ANIMAL #1:Type of animal:________________

Age in human years:____________

Animal's sex:__________________

Describe their personalities by listing 3 or more traits:

________________________________

________________________________

________________________________

ANIMAL #2 Type of animal:________________

Age in human years:__________________

Animal's sex:_______________________

Describe their personalities by listing 3 or more traits:

________________________________

________________________________

________________________________

**Step 3**: The animals are having a conversation. What are they saying to each other? Indicate the sequence with the numbers of the animals, #1 and #2.

**Step 4**: What were the animals doing and saying before the conversation just recorded?

**Step 5**: What did your animals do and say after the initial conversation?

______________________________________________________________________

______________________________________________________________________

______________________________________________________________________

______________________________________________________________________

______________________________________________________________________

______________________________________________________________________

**Step 6:** Give a title to the story________________________________________

**Step 7a:** What conflicts are these animals experiencing between themselves?

______________________________________________________________________

______________________________________________________________________

______________________________________________________________________

______________________________________________________________________

**Step 7b**: What are the conflicts between them and their world? Elaborate.

______________________________________________________________________

______________________________________________________________________

______________________________________________________________________

______________________________________________________________________

______________________________________________________________________

______________________________________________________________________

______________________________________________________________________

______________________________________________________________________

______________________________________________________________________

______________________________________________________________________

**Step 8**: What changes should these animals make to resolve their conflicts?

______________________________________________________________________

______________________________________________________________________

______________________________________________________________________

______________________________________________________________________

______________________________________________________________________

______________________________________________________________________

______________________________________________________________________

______________________________________________________________________

______________________________________________________________________

______________________________________________________________________

**CONFLICT ANALYSIS BATTERY**



**DREAM ANALYSIS (DA)**

Name:______________________

Date:______________Age:______

**Step 1:** Choose an outstanding dream from the past, a recent dream or a recurring dream. Check your choice in the appropriate category.

____Recurring dream

____Variation of recurring recent dream

____Recent dream

____Significant childhood dream

(Indicate age of its occurrence)

**Step 2:** Make a drawing portraying the key transaction captured in the dream.

**Step 3:** Relate the content of the dream.

**Step 4:** List the participants and attribute three traits to each of them.

**Step 5:** What are the conflicts?

**Step 6:** What occurrences preceded the dream?

**Step 7**: Attempt to give an explanation of this dream.

**Step 8**: Do you dream a lot? ____yes ______no

**Step 9:** Please outline other dreams.

**Step 10:** Dreams are related to each other. Do you see any pertinent connection or patterns in your dreams?

**CONFLICT ANALYSIS BATTERY**

Adaptation © 1984 Albert J. Levis, M.D.

**HOUSE-TREE-PERSON**

**METAPHOR TEST**

**(HTP -MT)**

Name:______________________________

Date:______________Age:__________

This test will help us in a quick evaluation of your strengths and conflicts. Take your time and do not worry about your drawing ability. Do not draw stick figures. Please use pencil.

DRAW A HOUSE

Things you like about the house:

______________________________

______________________________

______________________________

______________________________

Things you don't like:

______________________________

______________________________

______________________________

______________________________

DRAW A TREE

Things you like about the tree:

______________________________

______________________________

______________________________

______________________________

Things you don't like:

______________________________

______________________________

______________________________

______________________________

DRAW A PERSON

Things you like about the person:

______________________________

______________________________

______________________________

______________________________

Things you don't like:

______________________________

______________________________

______________________________

Here you may compose a short story using the House - Tree - Person information:_______-

**CONFLICT ANALYSIS BATTERY**

Adaptation © 1984 Albert J. Levis, M.D.

**SCRIBBLE METAPHOR (SCR- MT)**

Name:_______________________

Date:_______________Age:_________

**Step 1: Make a scribble:** Holding a pencil with your left hand, with your eyes closed, make a scribble in the space below.

**Step 2:** Study the scribble and identify any familiar shapes. Outline each shape on the scribble with magic markers of different colors and identify it with a number.

**Step 3:** Below list the numbers and describe the items you identified in this process.

**Step 4**: Elaborate on the significance of these items for you.

CONFLICT ANALYSIS TRAINING



## Segment III: FORMAL ROLE ANALYSIS PROCESS (FRAP): INTRODUCTION

The third instrument of the training program is the **Formal Role Analysis Process (FRAP)**. In this segment of the workshop, the testee reviews tests to detect insights. The formal organization of the process includes several exercises of formal analysis and of interpretation of information concluded in a letter to oneself.

Information is organized around two issues. The two issues are: first, initial *feelings of powerlessness* and, second, *reactive needs for power.* In the testing we seek to identify states of powerlessness and relational strategies to get from powerlessness to power.

**Issue #1**: To find out about feelings of powerlessness, we check the following tests.

1. **Transparent Mask Test:** The first mask reflects power, as defensive cover-up. The second mask portrays true feelings . The third mask reveals specific areas of conflict.
2. **Balloon Portraits and Story**: The drawings and the story reveal the power structure of the family and the testee's position within this continuum.
3. **Conflictual Memories of Childhood:** The conflict of childhood reflects an experience of special relevance for the structure of the symbolic universe.

**Issue #2**: To find out about powerlessness to power mastery strategies, we review the metaphor stories. First, we detect the dichotomies, that is, the antithetical characteristics and behaviors of the metaphor dramatic characters that usually reflect the antithetical powerlessness and power alternatives of the testee's own mental world. Then we review the stories of the metaphors that duplicate the testee's process of getting from the powerlessness position of his system to the one reflecting power. Sometimes this evolution will be completed not in the first metaphor, but in the second, the third, or even the fourth. The approach to mastery and resolution of the metaphors reflects the internal spontaneous need for role reversal .

Formal Analysis of patterns proceeds by identifying the antithesis admitted in pairs of characters by contrasting their traits, then by summarizing the metaphor story in a few lines and by recognizing the particular story as part aspect of a bigger pattern that one now sees revealed in the sequence of several metaphor stories. Finally, the testee explores alternative ways to deal with feelings of powerlessness, especially using communications that help one to avoid the conflicts dramatized so well in the repetitious metaphorical transactions.

## ISSUE ONE: POWERLESSNESS

**Define Experiences of Powerlessness Reflected In Your Testing**

**Masks:** Describe the types of power and powerlessness illustrated in your sequence of tests. Usually your first mask reveals your kind of defense, second mask reveals true feelings, third mask reveals inner pain and also inner resources.

**Family Balloon Portraits**: Describe your position in the power structure of your family and how this has influenced your needs for power.

**Conflictual Memories:** Describe this or other experiences of power/powerlessness in your childhood and how it has affected your life in your need for seeking power or powerlessness.

## ISSUE TWO: STRATEGIC PATTERN OF SHIFTING FROM POWERLESSNESS TO POWER

**Review Of the Metaphor Tests**: Check name of test:

___ Animal Metaphor Test #1 ___Fairy Tale _____Short Story___Intensified AMT#1

1. Identify the polarity admitted in your pairs of characters by their opposite traits. If your animals are identical, then identify the traits of an opposite animal or human being.

______________________________________________

______________________________________________

______________________________________________

2. Summarize your metaphor story in a few lines. Identify the transactions of your two characters, be they animals, fairy tale, or short story heroes.

______________________________________________

______________________________________________

______________________________________________

3. Recognize the story as illustrating a particular relationship in your life. Identify this relationship or personal conflict.

______________________________________________

______________________________________________

______________________________________________

4. What general strategic pattern of arriving to power do you recognize in this story?

______________________________________________

______________________________________________

______________________________________________

5. Could improved communications have changed the outcome of this metaphor? What could have been the most difficult thing to discuss between the characters of the story?

______________________________________________

______________________________________________

______________________________________________

______________________________________________

______________________________________________

______________________________________________

______________________________________________

## IDENTIFICATION OF YOUR RELATIONAL PATTERN

Accepting responsibility for your relational pattern is the biggest factor guaranteeing your mental health. Honesty - openness is the opposite of defensiveness.

1. Being candid, identify below the metaphor story that best reflects your relational pattern.

2. How does this metaphor show a pattern of ineffective relating?

3. What relational pattern alternatives could increase your effectiveness?

**FORMAL ROLE ANALYSIS PROCESS**



**RELATIONAL PATTERN CLARIFIED THROUGH THE ANALYSIS OF THE LIFETIME METAPHOR CYCLE**

**Step 1:** Animals of the metaphor test (or their opposites) reflect two alternative ways of relating. For instance, one of the two animals may represent the self-sufficient, rebellious, individualistic, restless part of you while the other may represent your caring, responsible, conservative disposition. Identify in your two animals these two alternative styles-dispositions.

______________________________________________________________________

______________________________________________________________________

______________________________________________________________________

______________________________________________________________________

______________________________________________________________________

**Step 2:** In life we usually attribute one of our relational alternatives to ourselves and the other to one of our partners (spouse, parent, child, associate). Which animal do you identify with and which animal do you project on your partner? Elaborate.

______________________________________________________________________

______________________________________________________________________

______________________________________________________________________

______________________________________________________________________

______________________________________________________________________

**Step 3**: Now attempt a switch, a role reversal. Identify with your other animal and recognize what partners correspond to your original choice animal. Elaborate.

______________________________________________________________________

______________________________________________________________________

______________________________________________________________________

______________________________________________________________________

______________________________________________________________________

______________________________________________________________________

**Step 4:** In reality one pursues both relational alternatives and periodically reverts from one to the other. Maybe you recognize how you have felt and behaved like the one disposition when you feel safe and then how you have switched and felt and behaved along the other relational perspective when you feel criticized, scared, or in danger. If so, please identify your alternative choices making up this cyclical pattern.

**Step 5**: Now identify one instance of this cyclic switch in roles.

**Step 6:** Make a list of recurrences of this pattern in one or more relationships.

**Step 7: CHRONOLOGICAL LIST OF OUTSTANDING CONFLICTS:** List in chronological order other important conflicts in the course of your life. Underline the most significant of them and in the space below elaborate.

**Conflicts:**

**Step 8: LIFETIME REPETITIONS OF THE METAPHOR CYCLE:** Can you detect in the above list of conflicts the recurrence of your relational pattern, the one you identified through the analysis of your metaphor cycle?

**Step 9: DRAMATIZATION OF THE METAPHOR SEQUENCE:** Because our associations obey an internal order of conflict resolution, the sequence of your tests have the continuity of a drama. Review your test imagery and outline below a dramatic scenario. The balloons define the key characters of your story. The conflictual memory highlights the critical experience of the drama. The four metaphors are connected as a timely sequence of a three act drama. A.M.T. #1 presents the first confrontation, or Act I, the Fairy Tale and Short Story, the second Act, and the final A.M.T. presents the dramatic conclusion. Have fun putting the pieces of your dramatic masterpiece together.

ACT 1:

ACT 2:

ACT 3:

## THE SIX STEP FORMAL ROLE ANALYSIS CONFLICT RESOLUTION PROCESS



Conflicts are experienced as mental and social tension. Resolution of conflict, reduction of tension, is achieved through expression of thoughts and feelings. Resolution of conflict is desirable, it amounts to the reduction of tension, of unpleasantness and disorder. Conflict resolution is achieved biologically, spontaneously, unconsciously, through the experience of dreams. It can also be achieved consciously through creativity oriented processes by facilitating appropriate emotional psychosocially relevant communications.

The Conflict Resolution Process is an exercise of facilitated communication consisting in consciously pursuing the natural flow of our associations. Associations follow a sequence of formal transformations , which we have identified as the six-role process. This process, equally present in the realm of consciousness and unconsciousness, is a logical and biological dialectic pathway. It is the conduit of the emotional- social oscillation of identities between two opposite perspectives, that of passivity and that of activity. At the end of the six-role process, thoughts stop, as though the self has reached an energetic equilibrium. This usually coincides with less energy, less discomfort, less conflict. It corresponds to a compromise and a new state of awareness.

The following communicational exercise retraces consciously the natural mental back and forth process of the six-role mechanism. This occurs as the testee considers a particular conflict from its onset to its resolution. The conflict sets off the process and then the step-by-step articulation of thoughts and feelings leads to its resolution.

The six-role process is identical, energetically, to the phenomenon of a roller coaster up and down structure. The roller coaster structure provides a wagon with unstable dynamic energy that sets a car into motion. The vehicle oscillates back and forth till it returns to a state of rest, where the energy is totally dissipated. The six-role process is a universal dialectic mechanism, a pump that transforms energy as it carries the conflict charge along its three cycles of interconnected passivity, that is, suffering, and activity, that is, mastery states. The outcome of the six- role cycling and of the energetic transformations is reduction of psychic tension and the increment of internal order. Consistently , the six-role exercise leads from conflict and stress to insight, from emotional turmoil to emotional-social equilibrial state of stability and conflict resolution

## ABOUT THE FORMAL ANALYSIS OF ANY FORMAL UNIVERSE

Any artistic creation across any medium of the arts has implicit communicational significance. The medium of a composition carries its message, be the art form a musical composition, a dramatic poem, or a painting/sculpture. The creator-artist does not need to explain his thoughts and the personal significance of his symbolic world. Knowledge of the artist's personal background and associations about his artwork may be irrelevant for the appreciation of his compositions. Artistic creations as metaphorical systems of order stand on their own merits. Musical compositions, poetry, dramas of human relationships, and canvases evolve their own language of meaningful and totally systemically and self-sufficiently standing symbols. The successful impact of a composition depends on the formal relationship of its elemental components. Good taste is based on the art form's compliance with universal laws of systemic order. Greater the purity or formality of the visual constructs in the composition's symbolic universe, more clear and more pleasing the outcome. Henry Gorski is very formal in his choice of themes, symbols, color schemes, shapes, and constructions. His preoccupations spontaneously consist in a disciplined pursuit of meaning, yet intuitively Gorski is interested and gifted in another medium. He is articulate, poetic, philosophical. His statements about the canvases help the viewer to grasp the depth and span of the images as true metaphors of a deeper vision of the world.

## INTRODUCTORY NOTE BY HENRY GORSKI TO VOLUME VIII: FROM ART TO SCIENCE, THE HENRY GORSKI RETROSPECTIVE

William Blake's prophetic and apocalyptic poem speaks to our present age of all-pervasive dehumanization:

"My mother groan'd! my father wept.
Into the dangerous world I leapt:"

I leapt out of my mother's womb in the back room of a working man's tavern located in a steel town during a world war. My personal odyssey since that traumatic day encompassed half the spinning globe and spanned a depression, another war worth three bronze stars, apprehensions of atomic dissolution as a map maker, still another war which threatened one son, dealing with a severely handicapped hyperactive other son, etc., etc...

Painting and art became a defensive shield which cushioned the "slings and arrows of outrageous fortune." What these "interesting" times ("interesting" in the acrimonious sense of cursing an enemy: "May you live in an interesting age!") had wrought to my inner person determined the directions my painting would take. Interest in other cultures dealing with these inward conflicts and bogey men of spiritual undergrounds took me to Pre- Columbian Mexico, mystical Spain and most recently to Italy. The study of Primitive Art experienced first hand in New Guinea, the island arts of the Pacific, Australia and the West Coast, the anxieties of Kafka and Dostoevsky and the mosaics of Italian basilicas established my particular thrust toward expressing and revealing some dimension of the inner person.

A chance meeting, perhaps a natural gravitation, a confluence of opposite attractions (of Art grafting onto Science) has since developed into a found relationship. Albert Levis perceived seemingly parallel directions in my paintings as symbols applicable to his Formal Theory of human behavior-- directions of which I was not consciously aware.

My own comments on my paintings in the following text are, to the best of my memory, the sources of inspiration which motivated them. At times there may be differing, even contradictory responses to my work; but that is the multi-faceted nature of art--that it can present different aspects, evoke varying responses at different times.

Albert Levis in his formal approach to behavior theory, as seen and interpreted through the artist's eye, has enhanced the realm of creative vision which I experienced intuitively as a painter. His new dimension of insight fostered a meaningful relationship between the Formalist and the Intuitionist. This manuscript extends the frontiers of understanding our humanity.

Hamden, Connecticut    Henry Gorski
August 1987

**Cycle 1**: Explore the six-role process by seeking to resolve a particular conflict or conflictual relationship. Start by identifying a current unresolved conflict that has substantial significance to you. The conflict's intensity will determine the intensity of all the exchanges that follow. Proceed by describing this conflict and then follow the course of the six logical steps toward its resolution.

**Role #1 RO:** The first cycle consists of the initial stress or suffering, the ***role oppression*** state ,and of the first mastery response, labeled ***role assumption,*** which deals with the first suffering. Indicate in detail the nature of the stressful experience as it occurred.

**Role #2 RA**: Indicate your ***role assumption*** or response to the initial stress.

# THE GORSKI RETROSPECTIVE PROVIDES EVIDENCE FOR THE SCIENTIFIC BREAKTHROUGH OF THE RECONCILIATION OF THE SOCIAL AND NATURAL SCIENCES

The Formal Theory reconciles the behavioral ideational phenomena, the humanities - the branches of knowledge concerned with man and his culture, i.e.: art, literature, and the social sciences, with the pure sciences of logic, mathematics, and the natural sciences, the branches of knowledge based chiefly on objective quantitative analysis: physics.

To demonstrate this reconciliation, I have over the years collected one New Haven artist: Henry Gorski. Originally, I displayed his work in my office in Connecticut. As the collection grew larger and as I moved my practice to Vermont, I brought it along with me. Now it is available for viewing by the public as the **Gorski Retrospective Exhibit at the Wilburton Gallery and Forum in Manchester Village, Vermont**. The gallery housing this exhibit is the **Museum of the Creative Process**, the Museum of the Integration of the Arts and the Sciences.

The chronologically displayed exhibit illustrates the formal nature of symbolic languages: 1) **the development of a symbolic language**, based on formal distinctions within a universe 2) **the exposition of the language's grammatical rule as the principle of conservation tantamount to the conflict resolution process**, and 3) the **demonstration of the spiritual and identity formative function of consecutive conflict resolutions.**

**Gorski's language's alphabet consists of the formal transformation** (in the Pain-Things sequence) **of the mouth.** The mouth is presented as antagonistic and cooperative, in passivity and activity related forms (biting mouth versus eclipsed mouth, being kissed mouth versus kissing mouth.) **The formal grammatical rule**, conflict resolution, is demonstrated in the transformation and the upgrading of stress energy into order and insight , (angry and obstructed mouths evolve toward communicativeness, mouths appear and they open up accompanied by a handshake and eventually, a kiss.)- **Finally, the progression of conflict resolutions reflects increase in abstraction of thinking, that is, of meaning, insight, order, spirituality, and identity formations.** These phases coincide with life developmental periods, each with particular conflicts and resolutions. The following are three thematically distinct Conflict Resolution Processes or dramatic sequences displayed at the gallery:

1) **The Pain Things-** Antagonistic expressions from anger and paranoia progress to those of oppression and hostility and find resolution as cooperatively evolving images: handshakes and kisses.

2) **The Kiss and Crucifix Series-** Images progress from the sculptured kiss as a pure love form and affection to those of intimacy, shame, guilt, and expiation. Resolutions are presented through images of crucifixion reflecting expiation and Christian identity formation.

3) **The Athletic Heroes and the Illusion and Reality Series-** Images progress from power struggles in the service of metaphors (intense athletes distinguished only by their team uniform and individual number) to man accepting responsibility for creating metaphors (the shadow of the artist painting illusions, i.e., his symbols, the sensuous conflictual sculptured kiss becomes a trompe l'oeil illusion of the concept of love). The artist insightfully asks, "Is illusion the reality of being?"

The Gorski exhibit demonstrates the orderly predictable symbolic transformation process the energy binding, energy organizing Conflict Resolution Process. It presents ample evidence that ideational phenomena are orderly cyclic energetic transformations equivalent to those of the oscillatory phenomenon of the Simple Harmonic Motion of physics. It also shows that this process leads obligatorily to spirituality, that is, increase of meaning or internal order.

In the following pages, Henry Gorski's art work is displayed to illustrate the 10 Levels of the formal organization of ideas. The 8th volume is dedicated to the comprehensive review of Henry Gorski's work.

**Cycle 2**: The first cycle of stress and mastery response does not resolve the conflict but shifts social energy to the psychic realm where the conflict generates anxieties and defenses. Formal analysis shows that anxieties are unrealistic fears related to the initial mastery behaviors. Anxieties amount to anticipations of role reversal, e.g., being attacked, criticized, or whatever the initial role assumption conduct was. These irrational fears lead one to related defensiveness. They alarm a person to take precautionary and preemptive measures and protect himself from the anticipated trouble.

**Role #3 ARR:** Identify here your ***anticipated role reversal,*** your fears about others' responses to your original initiative in the context of your particular conflict.

**Role #4 CPRA**: Identify your defensive or ***counterphobic role assumptive*** actions or thinking, or how you dealt with your fears.

# LEVEL 1 Formal Analysis

$a + (-a) = 0$ $a \times 1/a = 1$
opposites reciprocals

An individual's ideas are formally related to each other, they constitute a totality, the person's Conflict Resolution Process. The elements of this ideational universe are formally related to each other as determined by the laws of mathematical groups: closure, associativity, identity, and inverse. They obey the law of inverse: Inversely related elements are either opposite to each other considering the inverse forms along the operation of addition or reciprocal to each other considering the inverse along the operation of multiplication.

Diagram 1: To identify a given system's inverse forms, we proceed abstractly along the inverse property of groups and seek to arrive at two sets of forms or related role states. Under the operation of addition, we recognize the state's antithetical forms identifiable in any behavorial system as the cooperative and antagonistic alternatives. Under the operation of multiplication, we seek to recognize the role's reciprocal forms identified as the system's key role's activity-passivity with each of the above systems.

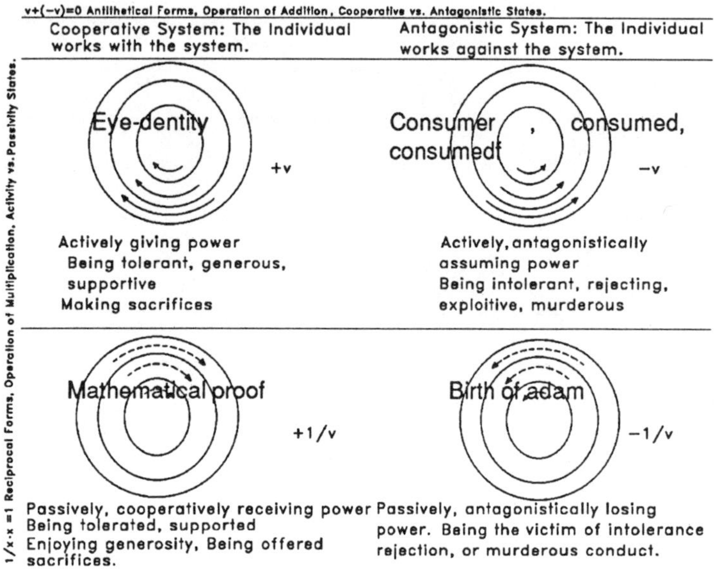


We may easily discern the inverse formal distinctions in the Gorski symbolic universe. They consist of the formal transformations of the mouth. The system of inverse forms of the mouth (angry-paranoid: *Consumer, Consumed*; oppressed-hostile: *Birth of Adam*; loved and grateful: *Mathematical Proof*; loving and trusting: *Eye-Dentity*) become the cardinal references for the scoring of the psychosocial game board. On this formatted gameboard, we may graphically portray transactions of the Gorski canvases and study their structural progression.

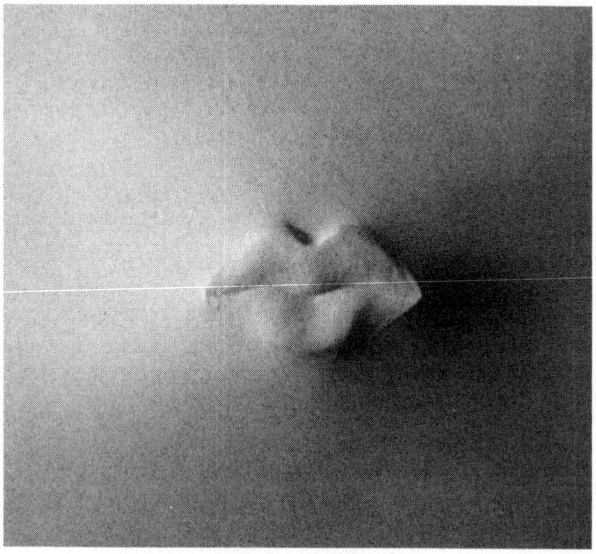

Large Kiss - 1968

**Cycle 3:** The first cycle of initial stress and mastery behaviors was followed by the second cycle, that of fears and defensive conduct. This second cycle of anxieties (or anticipations) and defensive (or counterphobic) activities did not resolve the original conflict but shifted its energy to the interpersonal realm. The third cycle consists of a setback, the passivity, and a compromise, the activity state. Conflict resolution is attained in this cycle. The setback is called ***role reversal***. It corresponds to the fulfillment of one's prophesies or one's irrational fears. The ensuing true resolution of conflict is called ***compromise role assumption.***

**Role #5 RR:** Indicate your ***role reversal,*** the outcome of your defensive behaviors.

**Role # 6 aCRA:** Indicate your ***compromise*** disposition or attitude upon experiencing the above setback by explaining what you did along the lines of settling your conflict.

**Submissive Cooperative**
The Mathematical Proof of
the Metaphysical Existence of God -1973

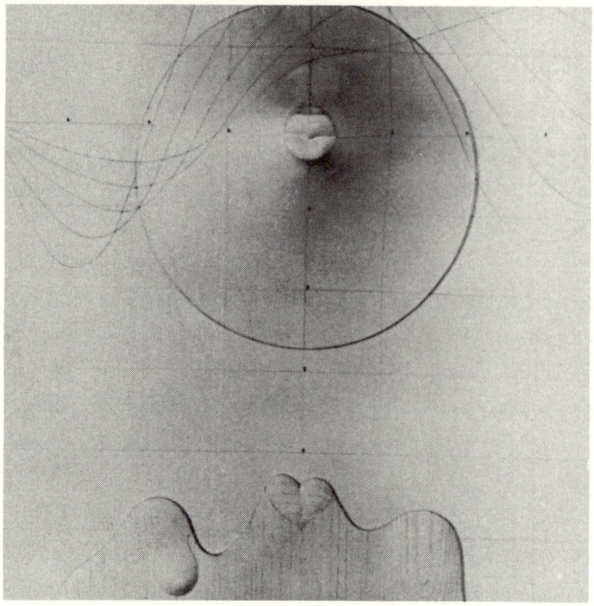

**Dominant Cooperative**
Eye-dentity - 1974

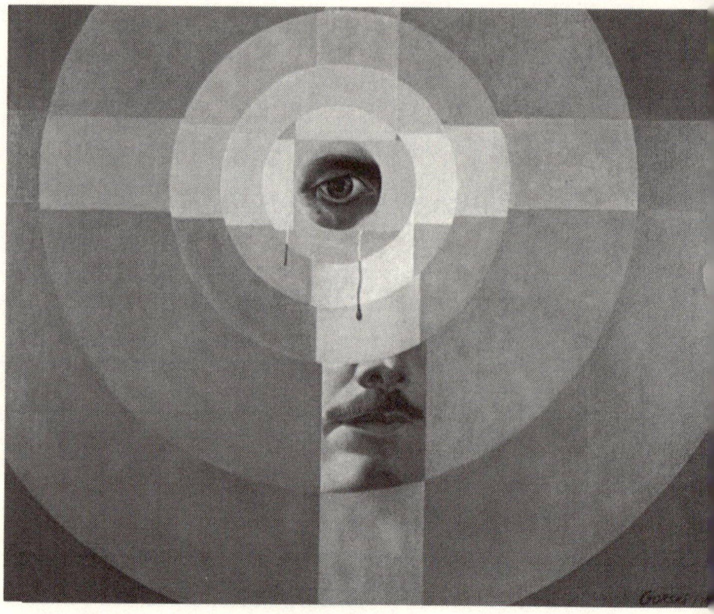

## An Exemplary Conflict Resolution Process

**Submissive Antagonistic**
Birth of Adam - 1967

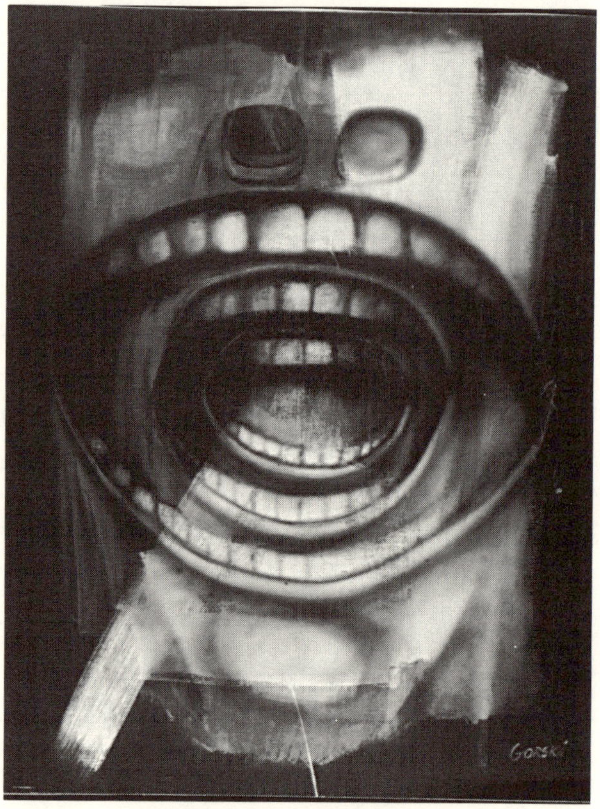


**Dominant Antagonistic**
Consumer, Consumed, Consumed - 1962

**Role 6b: Insight Feedback on the Experience of Conflict Resolution** In this section we review this exercise to become aware of its value in bringing about resolution of conflict.

**Step #1:** Identify how you feel now. Has this exploration of a past conflict offered you any relief of tension?

**Step #2:** Could this evolution of thoughts and behaviors have any relevance for you toward resolving conflicts?

# LEVEL 2 Variables or Construct Analysis

S, a, v, m, I, n, E

The elemental unit of a symbolic system constitutes a binary distinction or conflict which has measurable dimensions. Thus any conflict as a particular binary distinction corresponds to a clearly identifiable position in the conflict's continuum or formal symbolic universe. This position may be determined according to a number of measurable and formally related constructs or variables stemming from Physic's Simple Harmonic Motion. These constructs are: displacement (social status shift), velocity (behaviors), acceleration (feelings), mass (involvement), energy (conflict), etc.

Diagram 2: The three natural science constructs - displacement, velocity, and acceleration are defined as status shifts, behaviors, and feelings are portrayed as a system of concentric circles devised for the graphic portrayal of the Simple Harmonic Motion.

Any Gorski canvas corresponds to a relational form and has vectorial dimensions. The Gorski universe's scored game board in terms of formal transformations of the mouth may be refined by introducing the three key behavioral constructs: status, -S feelings, -a and activities, -v of each relational form: biting-being bitten, kissing-being kissed respectively. As an exercise of formal analysis, we may identify the evolution of the Gorski-man-woman relationship as depicted in two Mona Lisa canvases.The restructuring illustrated in the diagrams marks the passage from antagonism to cooperation from intense to reduced polarization, from role rigidity to role reversibility. In *Lady Bug* - 1967, seductive Mona Lisa is antagonistically dominating the men of the committee. In *Winner Take All* - 1982, a strengthened man, Rocky , is supportive of a mellowed, vulnerable, and loving Mona Lisa.

FORMAL THEORY'S ANTAGONISTIC CIRCLES MODEL

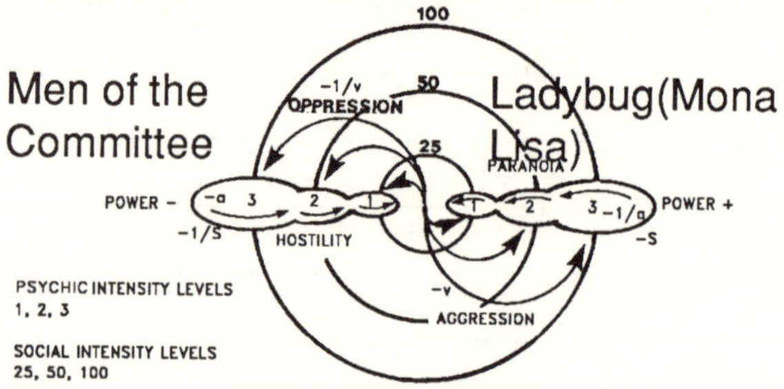


Ladybug - 1967

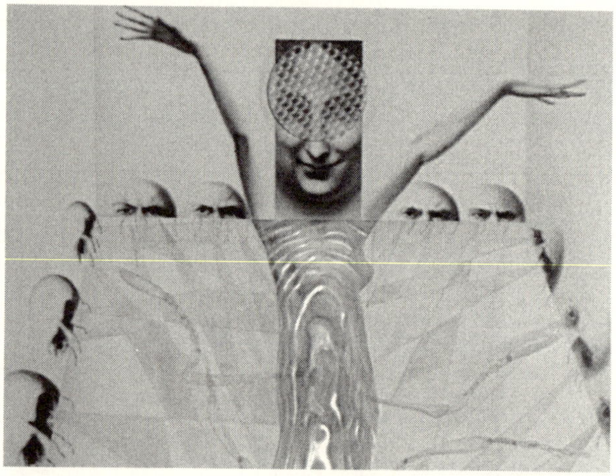

Winner Take All - 1982

FORMAL THEORY'S COOPERATIVE CONCENTRIC CIRCLES MODEL

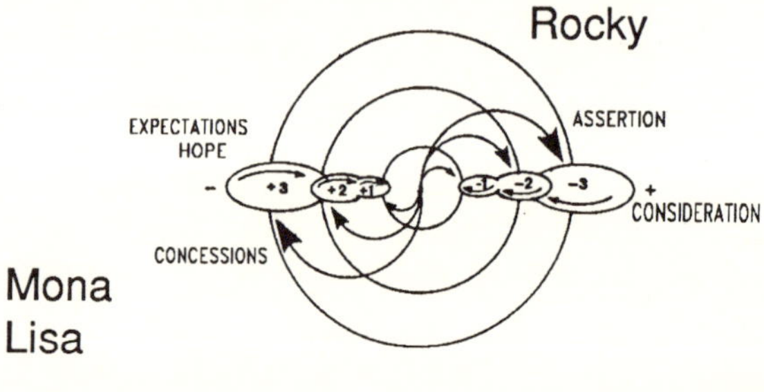

**FORMAL ROLE ANALYSIS PROCESS**

**KNOW THYSELF LETTER**

Name:____________________
Date:___________Age:______

**Step #1**: Correspond with a good old friend of yours, somebody you truly trust, and review confidentially your feelings about your testing experience. Review what dramatic material has emerged about yourself through your metaphor stories, and confide if this experience has touched you and why.

# LEVEL 3 Energetic Induction Analysis

$E = F \times S = (m \times m)/l^2 \times S$

Conflicts are energetic quantities whose intensity is determined as the product of the subject's dependency needs (F or a) times this subject's displacement(S) from his/her equilibrial or rest position.

In two Gorski canvases we see two equivalent states of conflict, one based on feelings of oppression and hostility, the other based on feelings of aggression and guilt.

Energy of conflict in *Homage to Kafka I* is yielded by the product of deviation to powerlessness (-1/S) times hostility experienced (-a), (which is equal to the transformation of his suppressed energy needs).

Energy of conflict in *Figure with Vectors* is yielded by the product of deviation to power (feminine kissing mouth) times guilt experienced (-1/a which is equal to the transformation of admitted but forbidden dependency needs).

Diagram 3: To identify the conflict-energy state presented in a painting or an image, we consider the figure's power status and related feelings. In the Gorski paintings, the relative position of power is determined by the absence or presence of the mouth in the canvas. Feelings are revealed through secondary symbolism, the eyes and the multiple arms reflect hostility, the vectors of internal tension reflect guilt.

Depiction of oppression and hostility

Homage to Kafka I - 1967

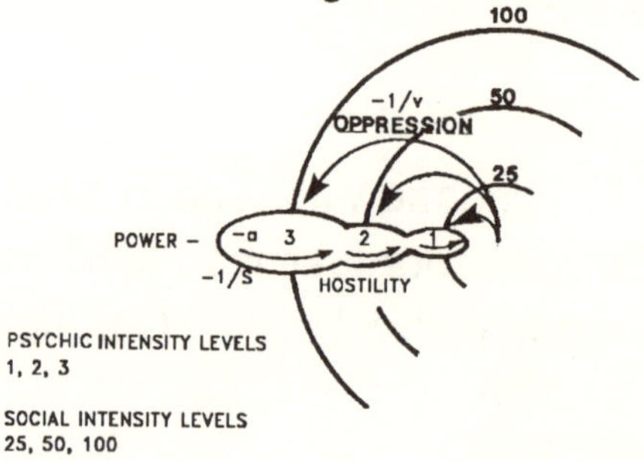


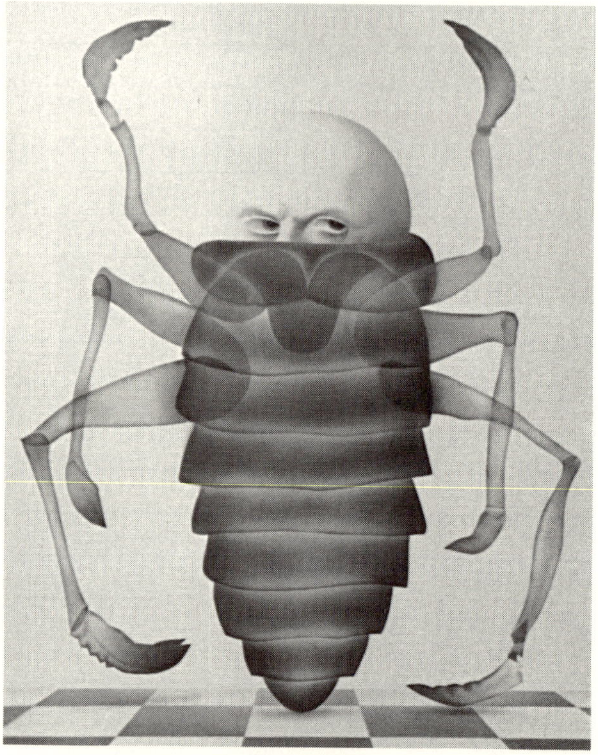

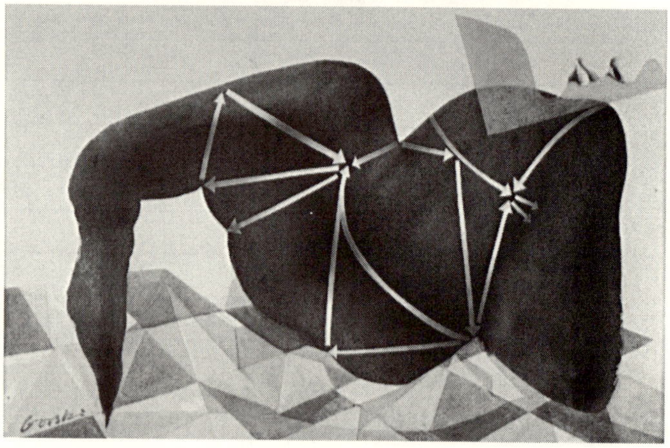

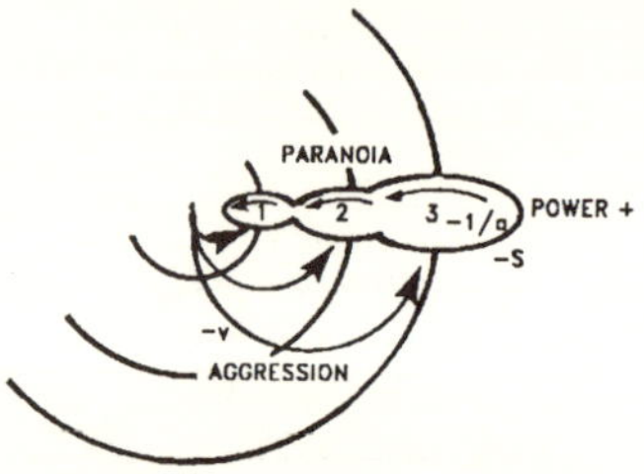


Figure with Vectors - 1967

Depiction of aggression and guilt

**Step #2**: Share your reflections about how you wish to modify your way of relating or communicating so that you can be overall better adjusted.

**Step #3**: Have you been honest in your communication with your friend? If not, why?

# LEVEL 4 Energetic Conservation or Modalities Intertransformation Analysis

$$E_{total} = E_{kinetic} + E_{dynamic} + E_{momentum}$$
$$E_{total} = E_{social} + E_{psychic} + E_{biological}$$

Energy of the Simple Harmonic Motion and of the Conflict Resolution Process is conserved through the oscillatory intertransformation of energetic modalities. In the inorganic world, progressively energy is downgraded into entropy. In the biological world, as in the process of photosynthesis, energy is captured and upgraded into meaning, endelechy or spirituality. The oscillatory process continues ad infinitum until all unstable forms of energy are dissipated or converted into stable and internalized energetic forms .

ENERGETIC FORMS AND THEIR INTERTRANSFORMATIONS

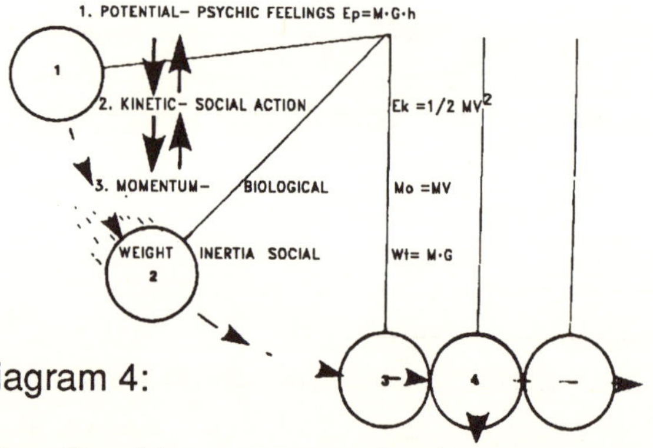


Diagram 4:

The Gorski canvases clearly portray the quality of the energetic states experienced. 1) Blocked faces portray psychic energy (equivalent to dynamic energy). 2) The broken gag over the mouth conveys the breakthrough of communications, that is, the transformation of psychic into social energy and its release (equivalent to kinetic energy). 3) The athletic heroes and illusions paintings convey dreams and fantasies, both of which illustrate the biological energetic modality (equivalent to momentum energy).

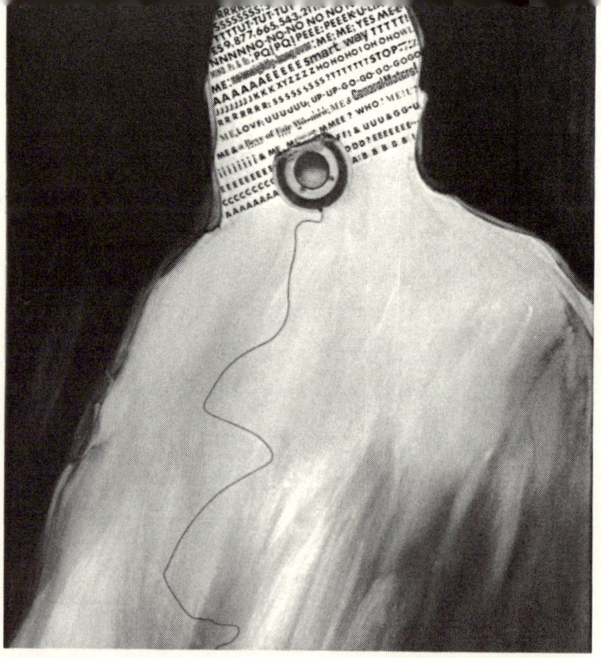

Man of Letters - 1964. Psychic tension

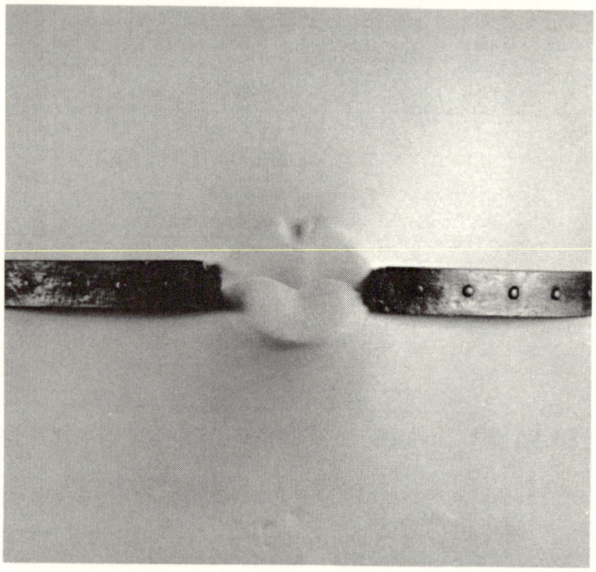

Saja's Secret - 1970. Tension released socially

Ice Gods - 1980. Tension experienced biologically, i.e.,in dreams

**CONFLICT ROLE ANALYSIS PROCESS**



**GENERAL FEEDBACK INFORMATION**

Name:______________________________

Date:____________________Age:_______

## Tests of Choice

Which of the following tests were the most revealing to you about yourself? Circle the appropriate score: low score, less revealing; high score, more revealing.

| | | | | | | | | | | |
|---|---|---|---|---|---|---|---|---|---|---|
| Relational Modality Scale | 1 | 2 | 3 | 4 | 5 | 6 | 7 | 8 | 9 | 10 |
| Masks | 1 | 2 | 3 | 4 | 5 | 6 | 7 | 8 | 9 | 10 |
| Balloon Portraits | 1 | 2 | 3 | 4 | 5 | 6 | 7 | 8 | 9 | 10 |
| Conflictual Memories | 1 | 2 | 3 | 4 | 5 | 6 | 7 | 8 | 9 | 10 |
| Animal Metaphor #1 | 1 | 2 | 3 | 4 | 5 | 6 | 7 | 8 | 9 | 10 |
| Fairy Tale | 1 | 2 | 3 | 4 | 5 | 6 | 7 | 8 | 9 | 10 |
| Short Story | 1 | 2 | 3 | 4 | 5 | 6 | 7 | 8 | 9 | 10 |
| Animal Metaphor #2 | 1 | 2 | 3 | 4 | 5 | 6 | 7 | 8 | 9 | 10 |
| Dream Analysis | 1 | 2 | 3 | 4 | 5 | 6 | 7 | 8 | 9 | 10 |
| House-Tree-Person | 1 | 2 | 3 | 4 | 5 | 6 | 7 | 8 | 9 | 10 |
| Scribble | 1 | 2 | 3 | 4 | 5 | 6 | 7 | 8 | 9 | 10 |
| 6-Role Conflict Process | 1 | 2 | 3 | 4 | 5 | 6 | 7 | 8 | 9 | 10 |

Overall, what did you find out that was of special value to you?

________________________________________________

________________________________________________

________________________________________________

________________________________________________

Did you enjoy the art work?__________________________________

________________________________________________

What did you think of the lengthy questionnaire test(RMES)? ________________

________________________________________________

Do you recommend this testing battery?

________________________________________________

________________________________________________

________________________________________________

# LEVEL 5 Conflict Analysis

a = -1/2 KS

Conflict energy may be defined in terms of motivational forces which are proportional and opposite to displacements from the rest state or status shifts. The rest state or state of zero distinctions corresponds to the individual's zero need, satiation, or equilibrial state. Conflicts vary according to the need realm of the equilibrial disturbance.

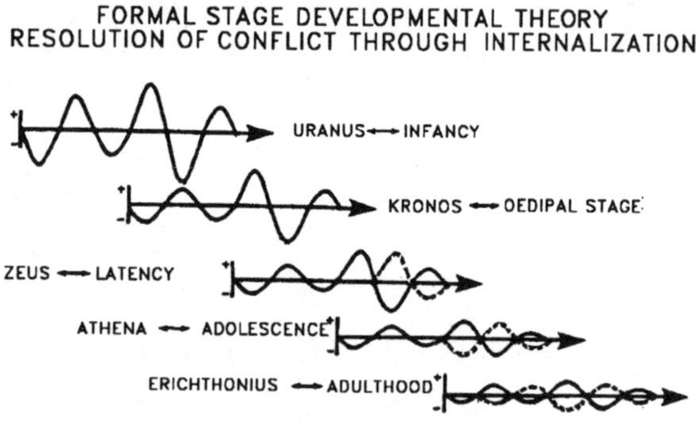


Diagram 5: Each of the Greek cosmogony's generations represents a particular conflict and resolution. The entire cosmogony set of resolutions parallels the individual set of conflictual experiences and sequential developmental phases.

Screening of the canvases for thematic nuances reveals the evolution of Gorski's symbolic preoccupations to reflect his personal life developmental stressors.

1) *The Abandoned Figures* - 1958 - dealt with the stressor of his autistic son's institutionalization.
2) *The Pain-things* series - 1962 - dealt with existential concerns about Vietnam.
3) *The Vestigial Being* and the *Heroic Athletes* - 1976 - reflected career concerns.
4) *The Illusions and Reality* - 1983 - reflect concerns with personal health and retirement .

Metamorphosis of Abandoned Figures - 1967. Reflects concerns about his sons.

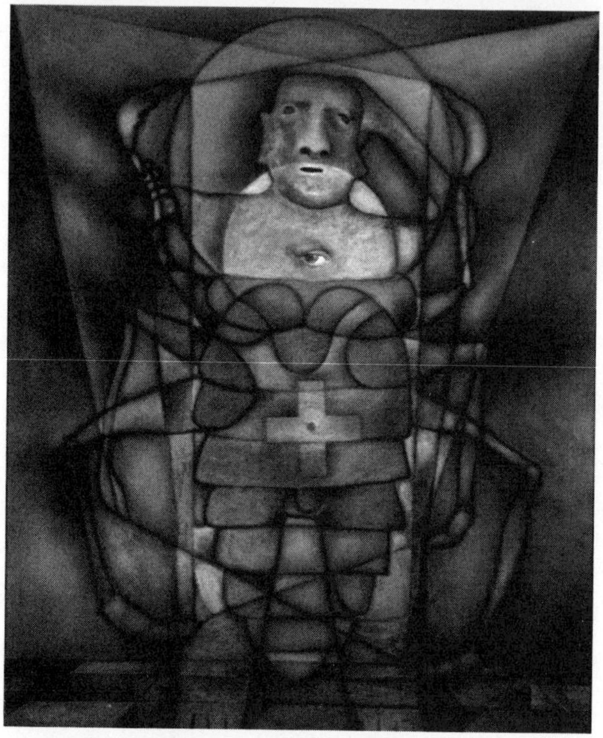

Vestigial Being - 1976. Coincides with career concerns.

Shadow Play - 1984. Portrays detachment from power struggles.

**FORMAL ROLE ANALYSIS PROCESS**



**SELF-ASSESSMENT OVERVIEW ALONG THE TEN LEVELS OF THE FORMAL ANALYSIS PROFILE (FAP)**

## Level 1. Symbolic Realm, Key Role

1. Indicate what is the dominant theme throughout your metaphor protocols

______________________________________________

______________________________________________

2. Transform the theme into one key word, a verb, the role of your system

______________________________________________

3. Recognize this key role's complement of formal transformations: the verb's opposite forms, that is the cooperative and antagonistic alternatives, then the reciprocal forms, passivity and activity states. These constitute your symbolic universe.

| Opposite | Reciprocal | |
|---|---|---|
| | Passivity | Activity |
| Cooperative | | |
| Antagonistic | | |

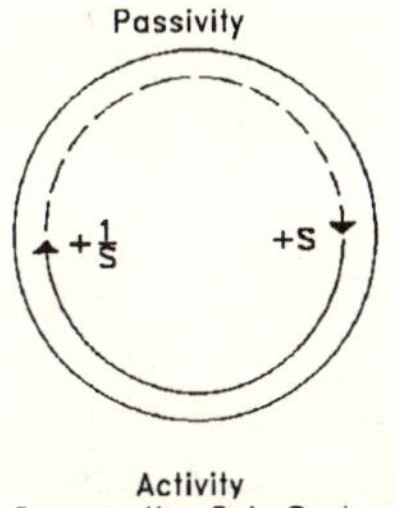

Cooperative Role System

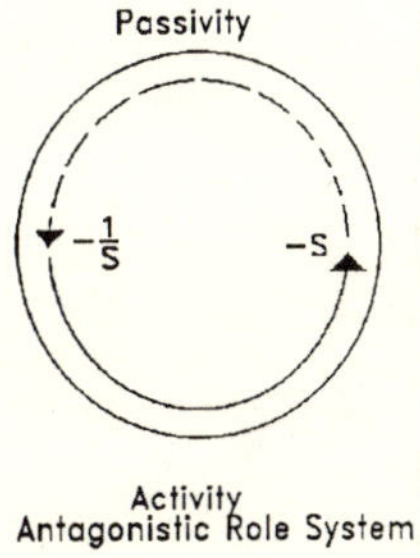

Antagonistic Role System

4. Decline this role through the six role states:

Oppression (RO)-e.g., being attacked/ cared for______________________

______________________________________________

Response (RA)- attacking/caring______________________

______________________________________________

Anxiety (ARR)- fearing being attacked/ hoping to be cared for______________________

______________________________________________

Defense (CPRA)- attacking/caring for others in advance______________________

______________________________________________

Response (RR)- Being overwhelmed by attacker/enjoying being cared for______________________

______________________________________________

Compromise (CRA)- compromising not to attack others/wishing that everyone would care for someone______________________

# LEVEL 6 Conflict Resolution Analysis

$$S = A \sin \theta$$
$$a = -a_c \sin \theta$$
$$v = v_c \cos \theta$$

The Conflict Resolution Process is an energy transformational pump which gradually converts labile psychic energy into meaning, endelechy, or stable internalizations energy. The six-role process consists of orderly, periodically reproducible energetic transformations, mathematically definable as trigonometric functions of the three oscillating variables: status, motivational force, and related behaviors. Clinically, Conflict Resolution Processes correspond to the syndromal sequencing of ideas and of behavioral phenomena.

THE SIX DEVELOPMENTAL ROLES

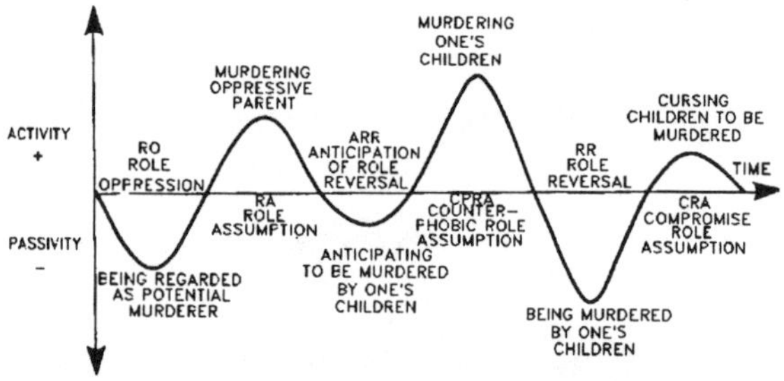


Diagram 6: The Conflict Resolution Process (CRP), inspired through observations of the Greek creation myths, consists of a sequence of interrelated role states or energetic transformations comparable to those described as the Simple Harmonic Motion (SHM).

Chronological sequencing of the Gorski canvases demonstrates the ubiquitous presence of the Conflict Resolution Process. In Gorski's Pain-things period illustrated here, we discern resolution of conflict first along antagonistic relations depicted with bug-like *Committee Men Figures*(1962-1970) followed, second, by resolution of conflict along cooperative themes (1970-1976: *The Kiss* and *Crucifixion* series). The antagonistic sequence, the *Committee Figures* series, presents resolution of hostility in that mouthlessness and manipulativeness evolve into handshakes and kisses reflecting the experiencing of a new attitude: trust.

Odysseus - 1964

Homage to Kafka I - 1967

**Level 2. Dichotomies of the Continuum**

Schematically draw the figures of your metaphors and below identify the two characters involved in the interaction.

| | Animal Test 1 | Fairy Tale | Short Story | Animal Test 2 | Dream |
|---|---|---|---|---|---|
| Schematic Drawing | | | | | |
| Identity 1 | | | | | |
| Identity 2 | | | | | |
| Conflicts | | | | | |
| Pattern of Relating: Transition from Power–lessness to Power | | | | | |

**Level 3. Energetic Charge of Developmental Experiences**

Schematically draw the Conflictual Memory and the layout of your Family Balloon Portrait:

| | Conflictual Memory | Family Balloon Portrait |
|---|---|---|
| Schematic Drawing | | |
| Most Significant Persons | | |
| Area of Social Displacement | | |
| Feelings Generated in Experience | | |
| Dependency Needs: Investment | | |

The Committee - 1965

5% - 1969

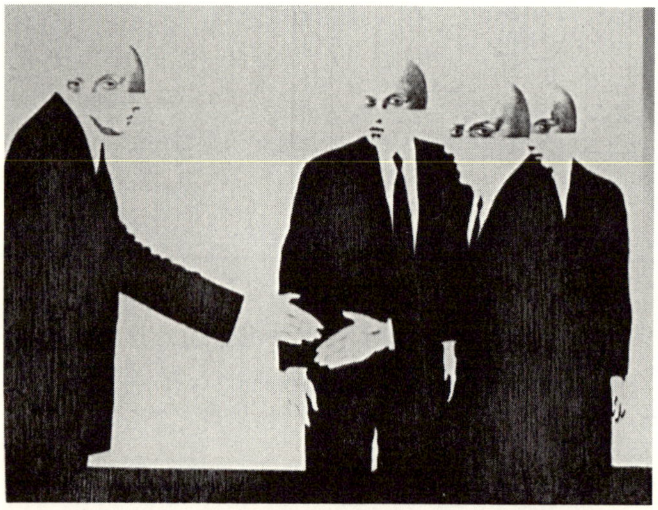

The Committee Revisited - 1971

The Game - 1973

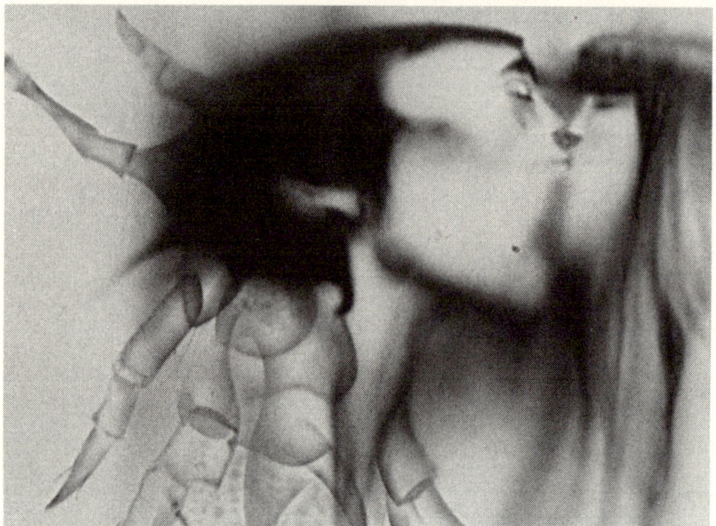

Love Bugs I - 1974

Love Bugs II - 1974

## Level 4. Evaluation of Communicational Style and of Energetic Intertransformations

1. Size differential of the two animals in Animal Metaphor Test #1:

___equal ___moderately unequal ___very unequal

2. Mutual orientation of FIGURES:AMT#1:___, AMT#2:___, Fairy Tale:___, Short Story:___(Place orientation number in space next to test title.)

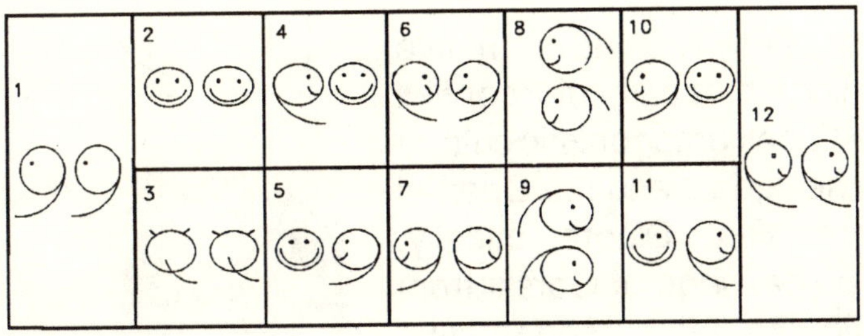


3. The distance between AMT #1 animals (alienation)

___small ___medium ___large

4. Number of blanks completed in the AMT #1 form out of a total of 14:

______________________________________________

5. Intensity of investment in the completion of the protocols (mass): ___mild ___medium ___intense

6. Cultural (ethnic) influence: __Oriental __Judaic __Latin __Greek

______________________________other

## Level 5. Areas of Conflictual Fixation of Energy

__interpersonal power __control of anger __loss of self-control __need for attention __sexuality __excessive need of food, alcohol, drugs, gambling __vision, voyeurism, exhibitionism __jealousy, ___envy __lying __distrust __fears of leaving home______________________other

## The Cooperative Sequence - 1968-76

The second sequence proceeds from the pure form of the kiss to the experiencing of guilt related to sexuality through to the formation of a Christian identity. In this progression, the kiss is followed by scenes of intimacy then of passion followed by a series of crucifixion paintings.

Diagram 7: Cultures are seen as normative environments which foster particular conflict resolutions. The Greek antagonistic culture is contrasted to the Judaic and the Oriental cooperative alternatives. Diagramatically, we may depict the passage of Gorski from the antagonistic to the cooperative sequence as analogous to the passage from an antagonistic culture to one that is cooperative.

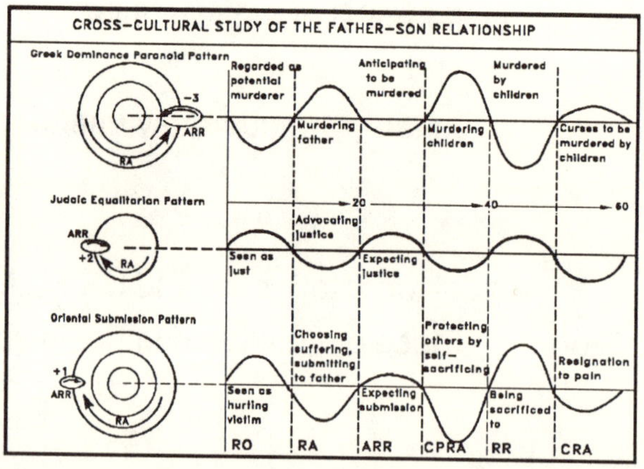


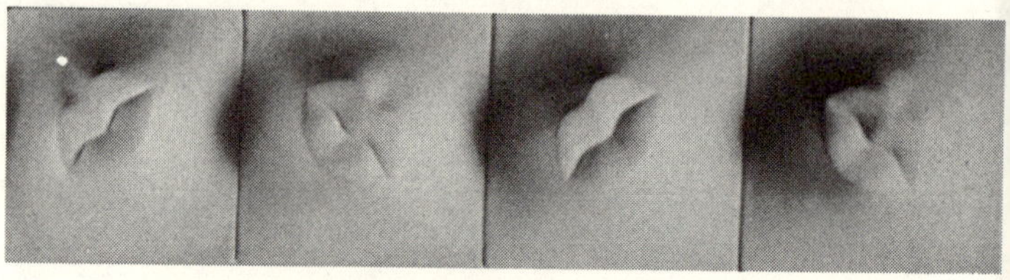

Alliterative Obsessions - 1973

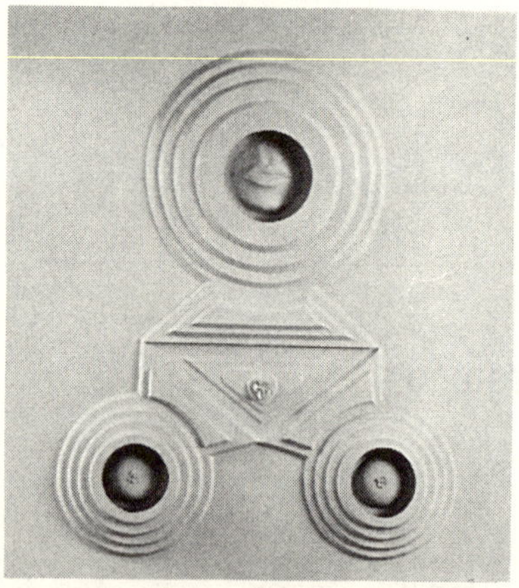

Hyperbolic Bride - 1969

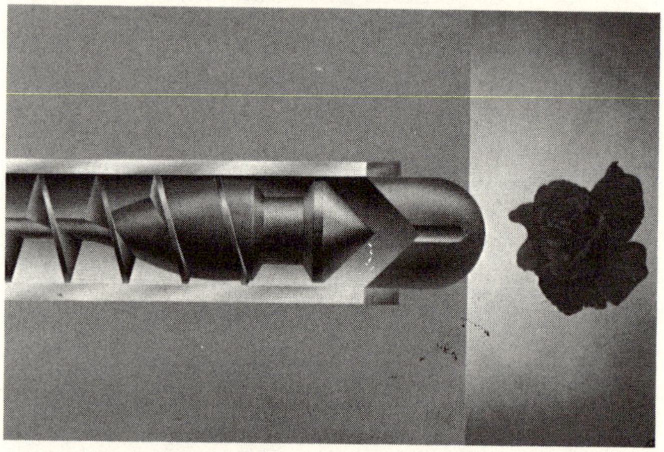

The Rape of the Rose - 1973

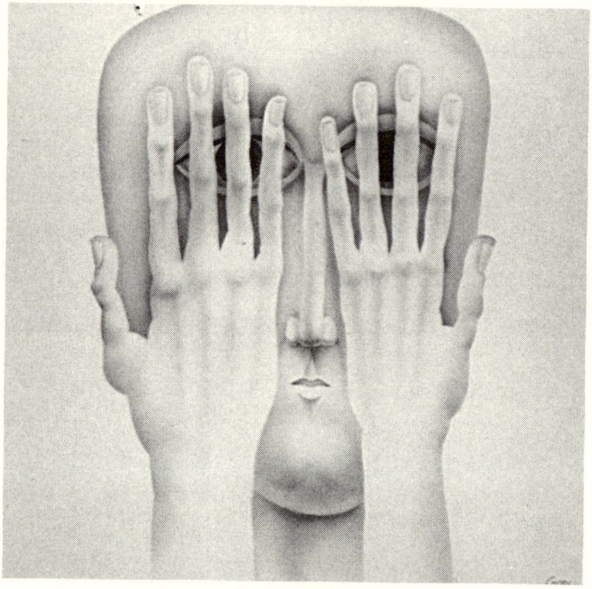

Nowhere to Hide - 1974

Crucifixion - 1974

**Level 6. Conflict Resolution Process**

Insert a succinct version of the dialogue of your AMT #1:

1st statement (RO): ______________________________

1st response (RA): ______________________________

2nd statement (ARR): ______________________________

2nd response (CPRA): ______________________________

3rd statement (RR): ______________________________

3rd response (CRA): ______________________________

Outcome of the dialogue: _____ reduced conflict _____ increased conflict

Your feedback responses to the testing:
__SC friendly __DC responsible __SA snide, evasive __DA arrogant

**Level 7. Graphic Analysis of Your AMT #1**

Insert the names of the animals, their attributes and related feelings:

Animal #1
Name: ______________
Gender: ______________
Age: ______________
Traits: ______________
______________
______________

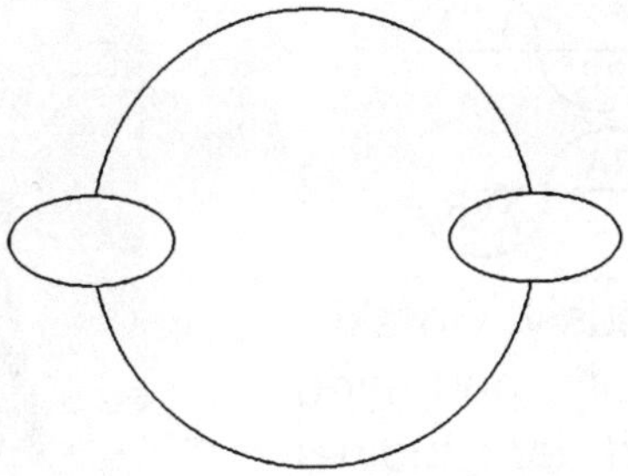

Animal #2
Name: ______________
Gender: ______________
Age: ______________
Traits: ______________
______________
______________
____

Insert declined role states along the diagram's role states.

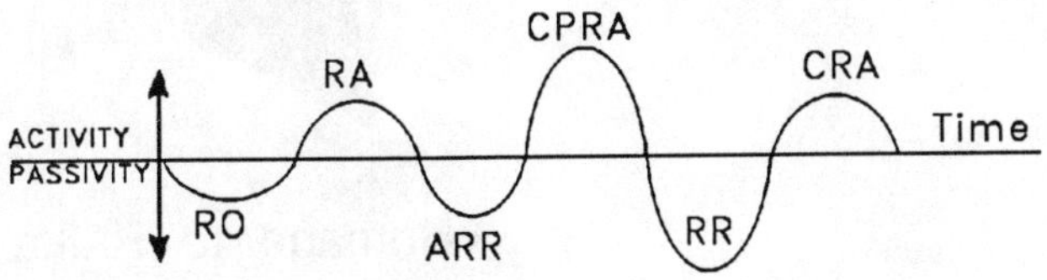

# LEVEL 7 Graphic Analysis

Conflict states and processes may be portrayed graphically.

*The structural portrayal* consists of vectorial depiction of social displacements (v) and emotional forces (a) on a system of concentric circles and ellipses (S).

*The longitudinal portrayal* consists of sinusoidal curves depicting the trigonometric variations of the interrelated variables as function of time. The vertical axis represents the intensity of the activity-passivity role states, be that in terms of social shifts, of emotions, or of behaviors.

THE STRUCTURAL DIAGRAM

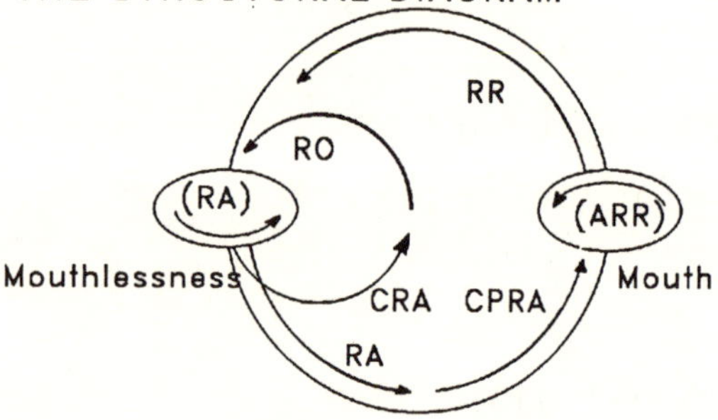


THE LONGITUDINAL DIAGRAM

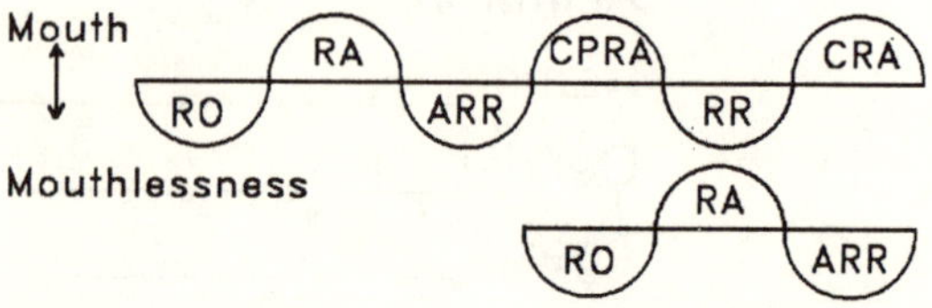


Diagram 8: As shown previously, Gorski's art work may be graphically portrayed through both structural and longitudinal diagrams. The structural and the longitudinal diagrams may be illustrated by positioning respectively mouthlessness in a position of passivity and mouths in a position of activity.

Homage to Kafka Series - 1968: Man 's oppression or mouthlessness (Role Oppression - RO) is offset by his manipulativeness (hostility)
(Role Assumption - RA).

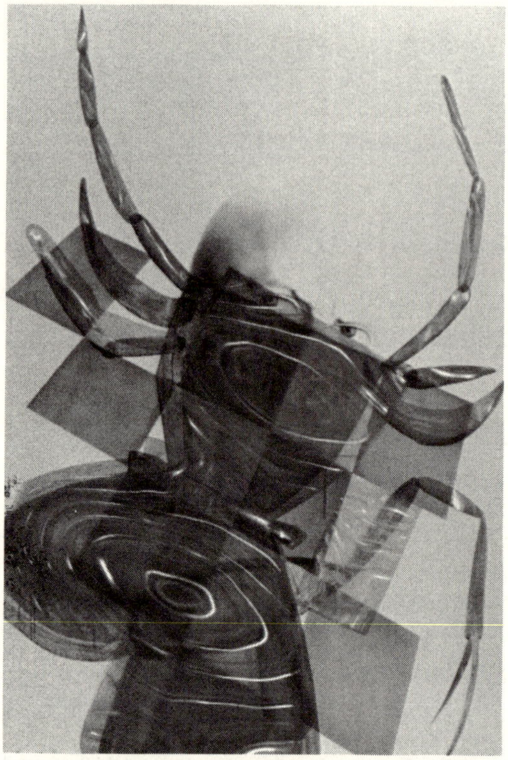

Homage to Kafka Series - 1968: The attractive feminine mouth indicative of power (RA) is extended with prehensile hairy prongs(CPRA).

**Level 8: Identifying Your Relational Modality by Averaging Your Score from the Relational Scales and Subscales of the RMES**

**For each subscale, enter here impressionistically the score of the average deviation**

| | RECESSIVITY | | | DOMINANCE | | |
|---|---|---|---|---|---|---|
| | -3 | -2 | -1 | +1 | +2 | +3 |
| **DC dominant cooperative** | | | | | | |
| Leadership........................................................ | | | | | | |
| Competitiveness and dominance........................ | | | | | | |
| Personal discomfort and sensitivities................... | | | | | | |
| Defensiveness and lack of compassion............... | | | | | | |
| **DA dominant antagonistic(1)** | | | | | | |
| Distrust............................................................. | | | | | | |
| Provocativeness with some deference to others... | | | | | | |
| Dominance........................................................ | | | | | | |
| Intensity in sensitivities and responses................ | | | | | | |
| Explosiveness.................................................... | | | | | | |
| **DH dominant antagonistic (2)** | | | | | | |
| Established oppositionality................................. | | | | | | |
| Arrogance......................................................... | | | | | | |
| Provocativeness and indifference to others' feelings................................................ | | | | | | |
| Negative to counseling and communication......... | | | | | | |

**For submissive behaviors, the direction of scoring positive and negative numbers is reversed here. You place positive scores on the left and negative scores on the right**

| | RECESSIVITY | | | DOMINANCE | | |
|---|---|---|---|---|---|---|
| | +3 | +2 | +1 | -1 | -2 | -3 |
| **SC submissive cooperative** | | | | | | |
| Cooperation, trust.............................................. | | | | | | |
| Compassion, considerateness........................... | | | | | | |
| Respect for limits............................................... | | | | | | |
| Recessivity........................................................ | | | | | | |
| **SA submissive antagonistic** | | | | | | |
| Communicational restraint................................. | | | | | | |
| Worthlessness, inferiority.................................. | | | | | | |
| Resignation without hostility.............................. | | | | | | |
| Resignation with hostility................................... | | | | | | |
| Hostility............................................................. | | | | | | |

**To detect your relational profile, draw a line connecting the average scores along the length of the scoring colimn.**

# LEVEL 8 Relational Modality Analysis

We distinguish four formal syndromal structural or relational modalities. The four formal syndromal alternatives are: subordinacy,cooperative and antagonistic; dominance, cooperative and antagonistic.

Diagram 9: The concentric circles grid may be replaced by a concentric squares grid, which also represents a bipolar field. The square's four corners simultaneously present all four relational modalities, the cooperative and the antagonistic modalities at the same time. The upper side illustrates energy flow in the clockwise(cooperative) fashion, while the lower side illustrates the flow in the counterclockwise (antagonistic) fashion.

THE FOUR RELATIONAL MODALITIES

Relational Modality:
Submissive Cooperative
Power:
+1/S
Behavior: +1/v
Non-assertiveness
Feeling: +a
Hope
Color:
Yellow

Relational Modality:
Dominant Coop
Power:
+S
Behavior: +v
Assertiveness
Feeling: +1/a
Consideratenes
Color:
Red

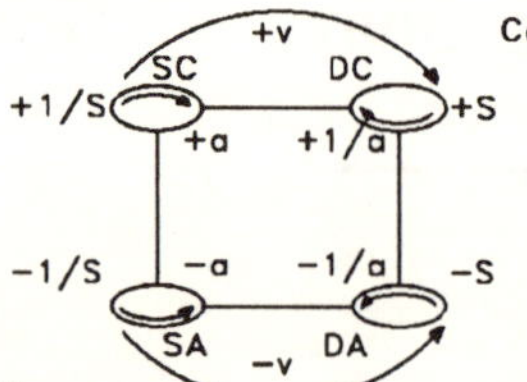


Relational Modality:
Submissive Antagonistic
Power:
-1/S
Behavior: -1/v
Self-effaciousness
Feeling: -a
Hostility
Color:
Grey

Relational Modality:
Dominant Antag
Power:
-S
Behavior: -v
Aggression
Feeling: -1/a
Paranoia
Color:
Black

Gorski's thematic choices reflect both an antagonistic perspective (hate-distrust) from a position of powerlessness (mouth-lessness-manipulativeness) and a cooperative perspective (kissing-loving) from a position of power (kisses and crucifixion canvases). The prevalent pattern presented in his canvases is his cooperative, self-effacing, hence submissive relational preference.

I Will Make A Man More Precious Than Fine Gold - 1975

Blocked - 1979

**Level 9: You determine the intensity of your psychic tension and the areas of conflict by indicating the subscale average score in the approximate line of the column provided. The psychic tension profile is seen by the line connecting the average subscale scores**

| Psychic Tension | -3 | -2 | -1 | +1 | +2 | +3 |
|---|---|---|---|---|---|---|
| Anxiety level........................................... | | | | | | |
| Family history.......................................... | | | | | | |
| Duration of disability................................. | | | | | | |
| Intensity of disability................................ | | | | | | |
| Phobic thinking....................................... | | | | | | |
| Depression............................................. | | | | | | |
| Degree of self-consciousness.................. | | | | | | |
| Particular areas of conflict........................ | | | | | | |
| Psychosomatic conditions....................... | | | | | | |
| Degree of relational stability.................... | | | | | | |

**Self Assessment: You have entered information along the four syndromal catagories created by the distinctions of dominance versus subordinancy and cooperation versus antagonism (Level 8), also along the several psychic tension items, which we summarized under Level 9 above. Here is an opportunity to indicate your independent impressions on how you see yourself along these dimensions.**

Indicate how you see yourself in the three social-psychic continua identified below. Score yourself in terms of frequency (percentile) and in terms of intensity (numbers ranging from -3 to +3) in the three areas considered. (i.e., you are dominant most of the time [80%], indicate how dominant you are [moderately, +2])

-3 -2 -1 +1 +2 +3

**Social System**

Axis I Subordinacy__________________________________Dominance

Axis II Cooperation__________________________________Antagonism

**Psychic System**

Axis III Depression __________________________________Anger

# LEVEL 9 Quantitative Analysis Through the Conflict Analysis Battery

States of conflict may be measured, that is, qualitatively and quantitatively determined. One way to achieve measurement of behavioral parameters is through formal analysis of standardized metaphor statements as this occurs using the Conflict Analysis Battery. To evaluate a symbolic universe, the observer must use simple analytical references - 1) Identify the system in terms of the formal transformation of the key role state. 2) Identify the system's Conflict Resolution Process in the evolution of the images. 3) Identify the thematically sequenced resolution as a meaningful evolution of conflictual concerns.

The Gorski retrospective study is a demonstration of the possibility to qualitatively order and quantitatively measure an artist's symbolic presentations. 1) Gorski's alphabet consists of formal transformations of the mouth. 2) Gorski's work may be categorized in cohesive thematic periods of conflict resolution processes. 3) Gorski's work is a progression of thematically homogeneous lifetime conflict resolutions.

The general progression may be pictorially illustrated in a number of distinct symbolic transformations which reveal increment of mastery, i.e., Gorski's handling of man vs. the game board. Man shifts from being passively ensnared *(The Snare*, 1969), to being trapped in a game (*End Game*, 1978) to evolving into a masterful player who is actively assuming the position of seeking to score (*Under the Hoop* - 1980). In the last canvas, the asphyxiating snare has become the hoop through which man can score victory.

The Snare - 1969

The End Game - 1978

Under the Hoop - 198O

**Level 10:** Insight

Indicate the six-role conflict resolution process of your key conflict (6-Step FRAP, p.64)

Indicate your awareness of your relational pattern (AMT Step 13)

Indicate your willingness to accept responsibility for conflicts manifested in the metaphor tests (AMT Steps 8,11,14)

Indicate your readiness to change (AMT Step 14)

**Segment IV: FORMAL ANALYSIS SKILLS TRAINING**
**1. Clarification of Insights Through Sharing within a Peer Group**
**2. Seeking Conflict Resolution through Communicational Breakthroughs**

The fourth part of this self-assessment process consists of discussion of the Conflict Analysis Battery and the Formal Role Analysis Process protocols. Participants receive information and support toward clarifying their insights. Sharing in a peer setting accomplishes an affirmation of the benefit of communicating feelings, accepting oneself, and receiving affirmation for appropriate growth. Active participation in this part of the workshop guarantees working on one's defensiveness, on clarifying insights, and on accomplishing communicational breakthroughs.

**Volume III - Other Forthcoming Publications in the Psychodiagnostic Field**

1. Training supplement A consists of a set of psychodramatic resolution processes that has been composed to standardize the interventions during the fourth phase of the training.

2. Training supplement B is a package of testing available for subsequent administrations of the battery of tests.

3. Training supplement C is geared for more in depth assessment purposes.

4. Training supplements D-E-F-G are modified versions of the training for its delivery to specialized groups, e.g., school age populations, organizational consultations, clinically identified individuals, institutionalized individuals, and those under rehabilitation. Separate formats are available for diagnostic screening.

# LEVEL 10
## Health-Efficiency Analysis

Efficiency = $n = E_{useful}/E_{total}$

The index of effectiveness or health consists in the individual's capacity to utilize his/her energetic resources, to convert conflict energy into meaning, that is, personal insight and internal order energy. This may be determined by the amount of insight derived (useful energy) from a standard task, e.g., a standardized battery defined as the constant total energy expended.

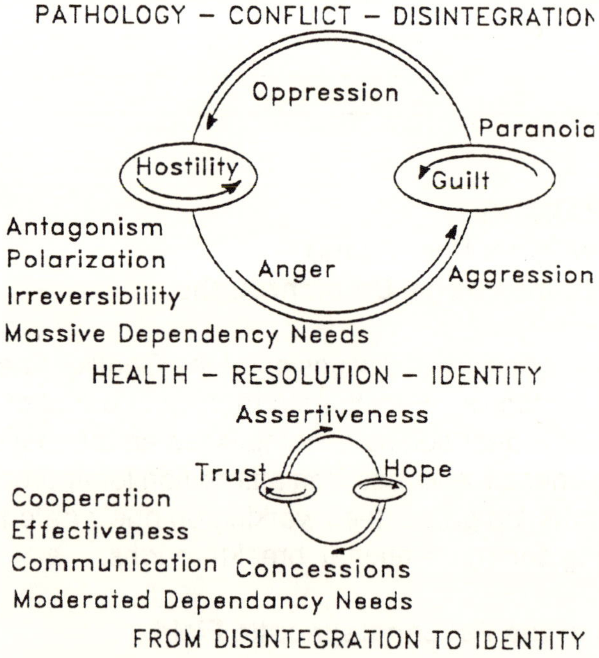


Diagram 10: Pathology and inefficiency coincide with conflict. Health coincides with conflict resolution.

Gorski's effectiveness or health may be judged as elevated, given the pronounced and consistent evolution of his early very conflicted work reflecting stress, anger, hostility, and guilt (*Composition of Stringed Instrument* - 1967), into his later work reflecting trust, love, mastery, caring, insight, and identity formation (*Manuel and Painted Bird* - 1986).

Composition for a Stringed Instrument - 1967

Manuel and Painted Bird - 1986